A practical gu
outsmarting over...

CW00701996

Argh!

Too much information, not enough brain

Lynne Cazaly

First published 2021 by Lynne Cazaly

Produced by Indie Experts P/L, Australasia
indieexperts.com.au

Copyright© Lynne Cazaly 2021 — All rights reserved.

Apart from any fair dealing for the purposes of study, research or review, as permitted under the Copyright Act, no part of this book may be reproduced by any process without written permission of the author.

Every effort has been made to trace and acknowledge copyright material; should any infringement have occurred accidentally, the author tends her apologies. Product and other names used herein may be trademarks of their respective owners. The author disclaims any and all rights in those marks.

Cover design by Daniela Catucci @ Catucci Design
Edited by Anne-Marie Tripp
Illustrations by Lynne Cazaly
Internal design by Indie Experts
Typeset in 11/17 pt Europa by Post Pre-press Group, Brisbane

ISBN 978-0-6482973-6-9 (paperback)
ISBN 978-0-6482973-8-3 (epub)

Disclaimer: Every effort has been made to ensure this book is as accurate and complete as possible. However, there may be mistakes both typographical and in content. Therefore, this book should be used as a general guide and not and the ultimate source of information contained herein. The author and publisher shall not be liable or responsible to any person or entity with respect to any loss or damage caused or alleged to have been caused directly or indirectly by the information contained in this book.

For the overloaded,
the overwhelmed,
and those who are just %$#@& over it

The LOAD of OVERWHELM

1

Argh!

The LOAD of WORK

2

The LOAD of INFORMATION

3

Aaah!

✦www.lynnecazaly.com

Contents

Argh

DEFINITION:

Exclamation

Used as an expression of anguish, horror, rage or other strong emotion, often with humourous intent.

Used typically to express frustration, disappointment, anguish or pain.

ORIGIN:

18th century: lengthened form of ah, expressing a prolonged cry.

Preface

It was all too much. A diary full of meetings, a list of things to do and another list of things that were undone at home, a family member in hospital, and I had to get to another hospital myself to have my daily dose of radiation treatment for breast cancer. Doing too much? What the heck, Lynne! Who are you trying to be? What are you trying to do? If only I could get a break and stop doing some things, and just focus on one. But life tends to throw us a bunch of things at once.

I'd reached peak to-do list — it was overflowing, over several pages — and my health was suffering. A diagnosis of breast cancer wasn't enough to ease the burden I'd taken on. I even took the option to schedule my breast lumpectomy surgery between three major work events. And I did. People would never have known. Prior to the first event, I'd been diagnosed with breast cancer. By the next event three months later, I'd had the surgery. And then by the next event another three months later, I'd completed the radiation treatment. I was just trying to handle it all. And it was all too much.

There was the emotional stuff of a health diagnosis with the 'c' word, cancer. There was the workload I was continuing with as I wasn't disabled or rendered completely incapable. And there was the information about all the things I was trying to handle; the health, the work, the family member in hospital. There I was trying to handle it all with the one brain.

Argh!

I cried. I sobbed. I snapped and I swore. And I didn't sleep particularly well, lying awake worrying – which made things worse. There was too much of everything.

I was absolutely overloaded and then ... I was overwhelmed.

But it wasn't too unfamiliar. I'd thrived – or so I thought – on pressure, deadlines and juggling things for years. Wasn't that when I did my best work? You know, creativity comes from pressure, right? Putting ourselves under pressure is how we get ahead, achieve and succeed. Right?

I'd felt a similar 'Argh!' experience when I quit a job after being harassed and bullied by a team member... one of the team members who reported to me. He'd pin little notes to my door each day so I'd see them the moment I arrived in the morning, telling me what I'd done wrong, what I should have been doing, and asking plenty of BIG questions about why I hadn't done this, that and the other and when was I going to get on to this, that and the other. He'd speak often with the previous incumbent in my role about how to strategise and work around me. He contributed only criticism, complaint and a daily air of superiority. It took me weeks, months, to recover from that job experience. I'd worked extra-long hours and tried so hard to do more and better and juggle everything, that I'd simply burnt out. I remember sitting on the floor in the lounge room at home doing jigsaw puzzles in a daze for weeks. Not eating properly, just trying to 'come back' from an overwhelming experience.

I'd felt 'Argh!' another time too ... after I'd facilitated 150 workshops for a client. It was a great money earner but it was too much. Emotionally. Physically. Psychologically. The organisation was going through significant change and the workshops challenged my facilitation skills every single day. Some days I got home just plain exhausted. Other days I was distressed and in tears. Still other days I didn't want to go back in there and face it again tomorrow. I was like a zombie. When the contract concluded and I took myself away for a little rest for a few days, I fell ill and spent all three days in bed. I remember just trying to push on through and persist to get to the other side of all of the pressure, workload and deadlines.

Come to think of it, I'd also felt 'Argh!' when I had to deliver a two-day training program for a bank. I was one of a group of trainers and over a day's 'Train the Trainer' training, we were told what to do and then sent off around the capital cites to deliver the two-day program. It was new information; I didn't know what to do and I had no experience with this technical content. I was completely overwhelmed from day one. It was intense to try and learn it all so I could deliver it with confidence and authority. We needed to look like the expert. And I felt far from it. I experienced a 'melt down' one evening alone in a hotel room the night before the second day of the program battling my way through two huge binders full of instructions and information. I'd also had to call a doctor to get some medical test results that day. Day one was a nightmare waiting for the doctor's call and checking my phone in the breaks, dealing with the training content and questions from participants and floundering, drowning in it all.

In each of these I was juggling and struggling and ultimately drowning under the weight of too much.

> Too much information.
> Too much to do.
> Too much emotion connected to it all.

Together it equalled overwhelm. And I couldn't make sense of it all at the time.

But we humans are able to get perspective on happenings in our life, particularly when we look back on them. It's hindsight, right? Things always look clearer with hindsight; '20/20', or perfect vision, goes the saying. We look back and make sense of what was **really** going on for us. What the conditions actually were. What we were really feeling and experiencing. But at the time, when we are IN it, we can often do little but just keep going, soldiering on and persisting. Surviving. Treading water or drowning under the weight of it all. It can seem like that's what you do or it's 'just how life is'. No one ever has an easy ride, right? Everyone experiences overwhelm, right? All the time, right? We all have to struggle and drown sometime, don't we?

Well, no. Not like this. Not all the time. It's not sustainable.

We can all think of a time or times when we went 'Argh!' Either verbally outwardly to the world – or to loved ones – or internally to ourselves. 'Argh! I can't cope.' Or, 'Argh! I can't do this anymore.' Or 'Argh! Why me.?' Or even, 'Argh! I can't go on.'

> We can't take it all in.
> It is too much to handle.
> We're thinking and overthinking it all.
> And we're trying to do too much.

When overwhelm hits us we can garner our strength – again – to fight the good fight and persist or we risk falling apart, falling in a heap, dropping our responsibilities and accountabilities and fear being labelled a disappointment or a failure.

No, we wouldn't be a failure. We would be human! But still we do it, don't we? We still seek to fight against our overwhelm. And try to win or beat it. Or hope it might be different next time.

I believe, and now know, we can make better use of our over-whelmed selves to actually outsmart overwhelm. Not so that it doesn't happen or never returns, but so we aren't so affected by it so frequently or for so long,

And this is what I've done over the past few years, applying and combining a set of skills and techniques that outsmart overwhelm from multiple perspectives. I'll make sense of them for you in the three parts of this book.

Overwhelm isn't going anywhere. And we can be sure there'll be a next time, possibly this afternoon or tomorrow or next week or ... who knows when. As 2020 and the COVID-19 pandemic showed us, the world and us in it is always at risk of being overwhelmed. What might overwhelm us next? And how might you be better equipped to outsmart it?

Introduction

☆ www.lynnecazaly.com

Argh! Overloaded, overworked, overwhelmed.

Work, information, emotions: together they're creating an overwhelming life.

Some of us get overwhelmed with possibilities or scenarios – what might happen, what could we do.

Others experience overwhelm as an internal emotional response, as they feel it inside of them. Still others recognise overwhelm as an anxiety response, or dealing with our fears, worries and tears.

And others are overwhelmed with the size of a task, the importance of a job or the complexity of everything that needs to get done.

Still others are overwhelmed with the job ahead of them, whether it's parenthood, getting their head around learning a new skill, starting a new job or launching a new business.

When we understand our overwhelm from a few different perspectives, we will understand why we find ourselves there. But what do we do when we find ourselves overwhelmed?

So far, we've been trying to end it, stop it, beat it, handle it, ignore it, restrain it, halt it, cancel it, reframe it, wrestle it, traverse it, tame and control it.

We've likely tried treating and regulating it, sleeping on it, counteracting it, dulling and numbing it.

The thing is, that's all been a little aggressive, fierce and powerful, and working against overwhelm.

What if, instead, we tried to get closer, to listen or to notice and understand overwhelm?

What if we tried to make sense of it?

Overwhelm is a message; let's listen to it and then we can outsmart it.

I've brought together three capabilities that will be too much for the overwhelm. It will outsmart it and make life much more liveable.

These are the skills and techniques I share in one-on-one mentoring with people who are business owners, entrepreneurs, trainers and facilitators. They're also the skills I share with corporate teams and leaders under extreme pressure to deliver and lead and change and transform. All the while expected to do more with less. And with a smile.

Part one helps us better understand and redefine the emotional overwhelm response rather than the blanket 'I'm so overwhelmed' exclamation we may use. You know ... 'Argh! I'm so overwhelmed!' We'll understand what makes us overwhelmed and how it affects and impacts us.

Part two goes through redesigning and potentially reimagining the work we have to do. If we can better handle the workload required of us and do this in a way that isn't a productivity quick-fix but a pooling of the most effective ways of working techniques, we can be all over our work ... rather than it being all over us. We will be able to reduce the emotional overwhelm connected with our workload. Overwhelmed by work will be a thing of the past.

Part three helps us deal with the load that is information. Information overload is a burden that continues to increase in our world and what we pay attention to or carry with us has a direct impact on our ability to outsmart our overwhelm. To be able to work better with our attention and information-gathering sponge can ease a load that can lead to overwhelm. The overwhelm associated with information will be in check.

In each chapter of the book there are resources and techniques to use and put to work to outsmart overwhelm.

There are additional workbooks, tools, videos and resources to support you at my website, plus you can join the community. I'd love to see you there.

The emotions, workload and information that contributes to and causes our overwhelm need not be an experience we just have to continue to suffer through and endure.

Join me on this practical path to making sense of overwhelm and thinking and working in ways that get the upper hand so you'll be all over overwhelm ... it won't be all over you.

Drowning In It

Overwhelm.

It means to bury or drown beneath a huge mass of something, especially water.

Alternatively, it means to have a strong emotional effect on.

When you see the usage of a word over time, it's interesting to note when it started, peaked ... and what it is doing today. Overwhelm as a word was originally at its peak in the 1800s. Use tapered off in the early to mid 1900s and the word has experienced a great resurgence of use since 2019.

The Cambridge Dictionary says overwhelm is a verb, of force. To defeat someone or something by using a lot of force. Alternatively, the verb connected to emotion defines overwhelm as to cause someone to feel sudden, strong emotion. And in relation to water, if water overwhelms a place it covers it 'suddenly and completely'.

At its simplest, overwhelm means to have 'too much to deal with'.

How Overwhelmed Are You?

HARDER
BETTER
STRONGER
FASTER

www.lynnecazaly.com

At the heart of much of what we do is a desire to 'do better'; in the words of Daft Punk's hit song, *'harder, better, faster, stronger'*. The 'do better' may be about a greater need to be able to cope. To not just cope ... but to cope AND grow and therefore handle more. This isn't a quantifiable 'more', but bigger steps, risks, shifts, changes and discoveries.

On that path of change we can get blocked by signs or experiences that say 'TOO MUCH'. Perhaps it's too thick a wall to get through, too big a hill to climb, too big a project to embark on, and so we can feel small or beaten or overwhelmed.

It's all over us. Like a wave, a rising flood, a creeping level that rises – perhaps quicker than we expected. And we are 'in it' ... over-loaded, overwhelmed and feeling snowed under.

Sometimes we can feel as if we have too much on and we can't handle it all. And other times we are given additional tasks, more responsibilities or we keep taking things on because it is what's expected (or what we think is expected). We can feel as if we can't get ahead. A sure sign is when we feel as if things are slipping through the cracks or that we are dropping things. Sometimes we don't even know what we have under our control because we can't even get to it or see it. There are expectations of what is needed in particular situations, and we can feel out of balance. There are times when we feel there is no time ... No time for us or for the things we like to do.

Some people talk about 'losing themselves' – that they are so busy doing things for other people that they don't have any time or space left for themselves. And still the world is full of great change and uncertainty, and it is constant. We may feel as if we want to get more organised or that we need to be better organised, or that we need a better way. Many people believe they are hopeless at organising their life or believe that other people are doing better. But we aren't alone in this. Feeling a loss of control or needing to 'work it out' or 'get it sorted' or 'get organised' is common. And when we start to get it sorted, we can truly wonder where to begin or wonder what we should be doing first!

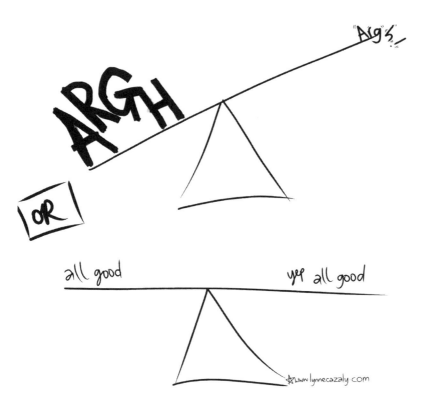

Overwhelm is a sign that something could be out of balance. Yet there are layers to overwhelm, and there are patterns that we can look at and learn from.

You don't need to be a high salaried CEO, an astronaut heading to Mars, the leader of a country or a scientist unveiling the latest health discovery to experience overwhelm. With the kinds of busy days we experience and manage to carry off with aplomb, the multiple roles we're fulfilling and the glorious aspirations we have despite these pressures, it's no wonder we feel the occasional – or frequent – 'Argh!' when we're overwhelmed with it all.

Everyday life can bring us everyday mortals a flood of overwhelm! When the challenges of our everyday life start hitting up against each other, stacking on top of one another and piling up ready for a pile on, the experience of 'Argh!' and then overwhelm, is perhaps the norm rather than the exception.

We experience many regular, now normal things every day that can contribute to our overwhelm. These '40 everyday horrors' can absolutely cause us stress. Tick them off! Which ones get you frazzled or make your brain hurt?

40 HORRORS

☐ Your laptop/computer freezing – *Really, we have to start with this? Argh! Right off the bat!*

☐ Slow Wi-Fi – *Urgh! OMG! Argh!*

☐ Screaming kids

☐ Misplacing your wallet – *Where the ...? Argh!*

☐ Traffic

☐ Being late for something

☐ Misplacing your phone – *Where, where, where? Hey Siri ... Argh!*

☐ Annoying co-workers

- ☐ Being on hold with customer service – *Argh! Don't even start with me on this!*

- ☐ A rude server

- ☐ Noisy neighbours – *Argh! New ones have just moved in and already playing a dreadful selection of music.*

- ☐ Waiting at the doctor's office

- ☐ Public transport delays

- ☐ Slow drivers

- ☐ When people let their children misbehave in public

- ☐ People cancelling on you

- ☐ Forgetting your password – *Argh!!!*

- ☐ Having to cancel on somebody

- ☐ People talking in the movies – *And. The. Rustling. Of. The. Plastic. Wrappers.*

- ☐ Have to use a public bathroom but can't find one – *Crossed-legged argh!*

- ☐ Delivery getting your order wrong

- ☐ Bumping into an ex

- ☐ Just missing your train/bus

- ☐ Somebody in the bathroom when you need to use it

- ☐ Checking your bank account

- ☐ Being in a crowd

- ☐ Paying rent
- ☐ Slow walkers
- ☐ Texting the wrong person something about them – *Oh, oops, argh!*
- ☐ Sunday night before the next week of work
- ☐ Someone trying to get in the bathroom you're in – *Argh! What's with all of this bathroom overwhelm? Also, I have a recurring dream about overwhelming toilets. Too much information?*
- ☐ Airports – *Oh, I'm an #avgeek and love airports but …*
- ☐ Not remembering someone's name you just met – *Argh! Memory, why do you fail me?*
- ☐ Facebook
- ☐ Bumping into an old acquaintance
- ☐ Going grocery shopping
- ☐ Knowing you're too drunk – *Argh! Hic!*
- ☐ Trying to get an extra drink before happy hour ends but can't find a server
- ☐ Holding the door open for somebody
- ☐ Cyclists

Source: https://www.theladders.com/career-advice/the-40-everyday-horrors-that-are-most-stressful-to-us

Spiders? So, there's no spiders there? OK. Phew!

Deep breaths. Just breathe. Even reading that list of everyday horrors is enough to fire up the overwhelm centre in our brain that prepares us to fight, flight, fright, freeze, feck it or fumble-bum our way through the day.

But hold on a moment; we can do this, we can. Let's get a grip on overwhelm and then outsmart it.

The Ladder of Overwhelm

As we experience and notice times when we are overwhelmed, and other times when we aren't, it becomes clear that overwhelm isn't an 'on/off' kind of experience. We don't switch it off forever; nor do we feel overwhelmed all the time.

It's like a ladder, rising above the overwhelm. And by checking in with the ladder, you can see where you're 'at' at different times during the day or during a project, task or overwhelming moment.

Here, I'll talk you through it:

ACHIEVING
PROGRESSING
UNDERSTANDING
JUGGLING
STRUGGLING
DROWNING

I'M ALL OVER IT

IT'S ALL OVER ME

www.lynnecazaly.com

CALM

CHAOS

This idea of a ladder gets us thinking about the different steps of overwhelm; the steps IN to it, and the steps OUT of it. The very bottom step is where we might feel truly overwhelmed; that it is all too much, we feel like, 'Argh! It's all over me! I'm drowning here!'

The definition of overwhelm is 'inundation' when it's used in reference to floods, landslides and landslips, where towns or cities are submerged – definitely an 'Argh!' moment. But we can feel like that too when we've got too much on or we've got too many responsibilities and accountabilities, or maybe the emotions of overwhelm are too much and we feel inundated, drowning.

Sometimes it feels chaotic on this rung of the ladder, and you'll often hear people on this rung say, 'I'm struggling.' Many people I've mentored, coached and worked with have talked about this experience – particularly when they're learning something new, taking on a new job role or trying to get their head around something. You might hear yourself say, 'I'm struggling with ...' or 'I'm really struggling to get my head around ...' There's nothing wrong with struggling, by the way. It leads us to create clever solutions and ideas, and it can bring out the best in us, sharpening our resolve or firing up our motivation.

But rather than saying, 'OMG, I'm SO overwhelmed!', if we can understand these different levels it will go a great way to us better understanding and making sense of our overwhelm; we can get some real insights that can make a big difference.

We begin to shift from a panicked and chaotic 'I'm drowning' to a clearer step up the ladder of 'I'm struggling with something here'.

Then as we make sense of the struggle and start to come up out of it or overcome it, we can get to where we're juggling. Just juggling! We've likely all been in a position where we were juggling multiple things at once: roles, responsibilities, duties, commitments, events, chores, tasks.

Leah, my physiotherapist, said that on the weekend she has to try and be in two or three places at once: a friend's birthday and an exhibition of her partner's art installation as a start. And then after that she'll zip off to play a set as a DJ at an event. That's some juggling going on there, Leah!

We recognise the juggle from a feeling of being split, our attention is here ... and there. You're working on this thing. You're working on that thing. Juggling is a place where overwhelm can still feel like it's on us, but we're not so submerged. Some people say things like, 'treading water' or 'keeping my head above water'. We wouldn't be able to do it endlessly, forever, but for a short time we have got a few things on at once.

Beyond juggling there is a point where things start to get even better for us.

As we understand the overwhelm better and make sense of it, something interesting happens: we can make better decisions, choices and ... progress. Even if we just kept at the levels of *understanding* and *progressing*, that would be an awesome way to outsmart and overcome overwhelm.

That's where I want to help you get to.

And yes, sometimes we'll be in 'I'm juggling' or sometimes we'll be in 'I'm struggling' ... but less and less often.

Ultimately at the top of the ladder is to feel like, 'Wow, I'm achieving.' It's a brilliant place to be. But we also know that always being at that level, at the top of the ladder, always achieving, striving, doing, getting, is not possible all the time. It's not sustainable: we can get tired, or we get run down. It makes sense that we might drop down to some lower levels of progressing or understanding as we manage, understand and outsmart overwhelm.

What I hope you'll be able to achieve through reading this book and applying the principles is that instead of spending more time down in the bottom half of the ladder, that you spend more time on the top half of the ladder.

We get to move from chaos ... to making greater sense of our overwhelm, through understanding and to greater balance and control. We may drop back down occasionally, but the goal is to spend more time in the top half of the ladder than in the bottom.

The Dangers of Overwhelm

www.lynnecazaly.com

Overwhelm is not just a passing phase; it's capable of causing much more in our lives than just the occasional headache, bad mood or sleepless night.

In the workshops I lead on outsmarting overwhelm, I get to hear from participants about the effects that overwhelm has on them. These are the things they experienced, felt or recognised in themselves.

They notice changes in their behaviour, a lack of sleep, waking at 3am full of thoughts, or having dreams about work or incomplete work. They dwell on issues and topics, get defensive and impatient, paying partial attention and realising they're not doing anything particularly well.

They found themselves venting to others, bouncing between tasks and taking an eternity to complete them ... or never completing any of them at all. They also noticed an increase in physical stress and muscle tension, leading them to want to indulge in varying substances to ease the discomfort, like food, alcohol, Netflix, gaming, gambling and medication. They noticed they began making 'mountains out of mole hills', finding that small problems were perceived as being larger. Their expectations then began rising, not just of themselves, but of others too. They reported a type of hopeless or lost feeling at times, often asking the question, 'where do I even start with all of this?'

A few of those effects might be tolerable in the short term. We've all had a tough week or a busy time working towards a deadline. We know what it's like to juggle multiple responsibilities and commitments, to 'burn the candle at both ends' or 'push on through' to get something done, handle an emotionally draining time, a complex and demanding project or a persistent and enduring problem.

Over a sustained period of time – weeks, months and years – this unrelenting pressure and stress, the overwhelm of too much of anything, can lead us to something we may not see until it's too late: burn-out.

Burn-out is now an 'occupational phenomenon', so said the World Health Organization (WHO) in 2019 when burn-out was reclassified not as a medical condition that you catch or get but as an occupational phenomenon. They explained that 'burn-out is a syndrome conceptualized from chronic workplace stress that has not been successfully managed'.

Boom! That's exactly what I'd been doing, several times in my work life; juggling, struggling and drowning for weeks and months at a time.

Work happens in our communities, institutions, families and households and can happen outside of a separate workplace or office or an actual paid 'job'. And where work happens has changed even more so since the global pandemic of COVID-19 made it necessary for so many people to work from home, blurring the lines between what work is and what home is.

Burn-out is where we're headed if we don't better understand our overwhelm and better outsmart it. Persistent, frequent and ongoing overwhelm puts our body and mind into a hypervigilant, fight or flight state. With little or no break from overwhelm, burn-out is a high risk for people who feel exhausted, are losing interest in what they're doing, are struggling to perform effectively and have a sense that they could do better, if only they could 'get a break' from it all.

The WHO continued their definition of burn-out as being characterised by three dimensions:

- ☆ feelings of energy depletion or exhaustion

- ☆ increased mental distance from one's job or feelings of negativism or cynicism related to one's job, and

- ☆ reduced professional efficacy, or the ability to produce a desired result.

Burn-out is related more to our work and jobs rather than other experiences in life ... and so it's in work that we can find some of the biggest contributors to overwhelm.

In the article, 'Burn-Out Put Me In The Hospital. This Is What I Learned About Healthy Work-Life Balance', Alice Merron explains how she was 'turning up and smiling' while in her corporate job but 'inside I was burning out and only just treading water'. She writes about how she would 'wake up exhausted, dreading the day, already stressed, with my to-do list already consuming my thoughts. I was overwhelmed.'

Merron had experienced a level of stress for 'such an extended period of time' that she 'had physically damaged the tissues in my body.' The stress hormone, cortisol, was weakening her.

She, like many others, understands how 'it's easy to lose yourself in your work in a culture that values success, achievement, and productivity.

'You might feel that pressure to push yourself harder and faster but everyone has a limit and it's most certainly not one-speed-fits-all.'

Her story highlights how what we think we can cope with may not be a healthy balance after all. There are opportunities for us to change how we experience overwhelm, change what contributes to it and change our responses to it.

There can be a quick inner voice, which might almost sound like a strict school teacher, who tells us to 'toughen up' or 'pull it together' when overwhelm rises. But we also know that stifling, ignoring and shoving feelings down or holding them back isn't helpful either!

Overwhelm that doesn't stop may lead on to anxiety, depression and other physical and mental wellbeing challenges. Researchers who studied the 'physical, psychological and occupational consequences of job burnout' found connections to:

Physical Consequences

- High cholesterol

- Type 2 diabetes

- Coronary heart disease

- Musculoskeletal pain

- Prolonged fatigue

- ☆ Headaches
- ☆ Gastrointestinal issues, respiratory problems and severe injuries and mortality below the age of 45 years.

Psychological Consequences

- ☆ Insomnia
- ☆ Depressive symptoms
- ☆ Use of psychotropic and antidepressant medications
- ☆ Hospitalisation for mental disorders.

Professional Consequences

- ☆ Job dissatisfaction
- ☆ Absenteeism
- ☆ New disability pension
- ☆ Presenteeism.

The findings of the research (by Salvagioni, Melanda, Mesas, Gonzalez, Gabani and Andrade), suggest the 'individual and social impacts of burn-out highlight the need for preventive interventions and early identification ... in the work environment.'

Ongoing and untamed overwhelm can become a kind of chronic complaint, like a sore back injured in a fitness flurry that doesn't quite return to how it used to be. Some overwhelm may always seem to be there bubbling, ready to rise up when something more comes at us. Sometimes people describe it as 'losing their shit' or 'on the verge of losing it'.

> *A meme says 'It's ok to lose your shit sometimes because if you keep your shit, you'll end up full of shit and then you'll explode and there will be shit everywhere. A shit storm, and no one wants that.'*

In his book *Brainblocks*, Theo Tsaousides says that overwhelm is making us distracted, tired, irritable, wasteful, unproductive, forgetful, unfocused, and indecisive. It causes our minds to race, our attention to rapidly switch between tasks; we don't know what to do first; we feel like we're being spread too thinly. And no one likes their favourite sandwich filling spread too thinly! Why do we do it to ourselves?

When we experience overwhelm in our day-to-day life, we can struggle with a range of responses and effects. Which of these do you identify with or have experienced?

Beliefs and mindset

☆ **Too busy with 'me'.** When we're locked up in overwhelm, we don't have time for others. Yes, we need to take care of ourselves first, so that we CAN have time and space for others. But how absorbing will our life be if it's all about me, me, me!?

☆ **Shame.** We can feel that because we can't achieve what we expect or what we are juggling that we are broken or that we are not good enough.

☆ **No fun.** We can lose our sense of fun and spontaneity. We're busy putting out fires in all corners of our life and our light-hearted laughter has gone missing.

☆ **Distorting reality.** Because we're under this sustained pressure, we can distort or exaggerate reality, be unsure of what we've truly got on, how long it will take and when it might be finished. We may overestimate, overcomplicate and over-engineer that which doesn't need it.

Progress and outcomes

☆ **No space.** We can feel like we don't have time or bandwidth for anything else and can miss out or become disconnected.

☆ **Procrastination.** We delay starting tasks, projects and activities … And may fail to finish them in a timely manner or when they fall due.

- ☆ **Indecision.** The doubt that can appear as a result of hesitating, waiting and oscillating among alternatives can be costly. Doubt can rise as hesitation or indecision continues in a state of overwhelm.

- ☆ **Closed off to new.** Our load is so heavy we don't dare add another thing to it. And nor should anyone else! Don't even think about it! But we miss out on opportunities, insights, experiences, last minute possibilities, invitations and availabilities, because we're not available.

Mental health and wellbeing

- ☆ **Inefficiency exhaustion.** Tasks, chores or activities that may actually take only a short period of time end up taking us longer. A lack of priority means we might pick up and drop a task several times, which is tiring.

- ☆ **Sleeplessness and insomnia.** Can we be so overwhelmed with our overwhelm that we can't sleep? We become restless and wake up every hour – not for a feed, but for some more thinking, overwhelm and worry.

- ☆ **Adrenaline fuelled.** We may appear and feel irritable, agitated, intense or impatient.

- ☆ **Short fuses.** Feeling frustrated, stressed and overwhelmed can bring on short tempers and fuses, meaning we can be triggered by the simplest of things and react in ways that are out of proportion.

- ☆ **Stern self-talkers.** And so, in times like these, who gets all the bad mouthing? We do! We talk ourselves down and out, abusing, critiquing and magnifying every little thing. We take our own inventory about what's not good, berating and reprimanding.

Effort and waste

⭐ **The cost of waste.** Living and working in sustainable ways is not just about physical resources; it is also about human resources – people. What is the cost of wasted energy, activity, attention and time spent on activities when you are in an overwhelmed state?

⭐ **It's all too hard.** Everything becomes an extra effort in overwhelm. When there's no space, and when we DO need to take on something more, it's an extreme effort.

⭐ **Inaccuracies and errors.** Working in an overwhelmed state can lead to making more mistakes which could be disastrous depending on the field you work in, the roles you have or the kind of work you do.

⭐ **Stretched thinly.** How much attention are we really giving the people and projects in our life when we are trying to do so many things at once? Our resources get stretched and our presence is stretched across many things, people, places and projects.

With these kinds of effects on us, it's worth making better sense of our overwhelm and working out how to outsmart it.

The Role of Sensemaking

Life can only be understood backwards;
but it must be lived forwards.
— Soren Kierkegaard

How do we deal with overwhelm and still fire up the parts of our brain that like to explore, experiment, learn and make sense? When we're overwhelmed, it might be easier to shut down, freeze or feel paralysed. For many people who experience overwhelm, they also tend to 'push on' or 'try and get through' what they're experiencing.

What if we could do something that made greater sense of our overwhelm, helped us move through it and come out the other side in better shape?

Imagine if we could 'unload' the overwhelm we're struggling with and as a result, our overwhelm dissipated, dissolved or just wasn't as overwhelming?

It was 2013 when the Institute for the Future identified sense-making as one of the future skills that we would require for the unknown world ahead of us. Little did any of us know (or perhaps this is the power of the Institute for the Future) of what lay ahead. In 2020 the COVID-19 novel coronavirus brought the world to its knees and added a hefty dose of overwhelm to our lives.

Sensemaking is our way of **thinking, deciding and acting**. Its history, meaning and use has been well documented in the brilliant book *Sensemaking In Organizations* by Dr. Karl Weick, often called the 'father of sensemaking'. I love his work! And even though he focuses on organisations, there is much about sensemaking we can learn about and apply to our own lives.

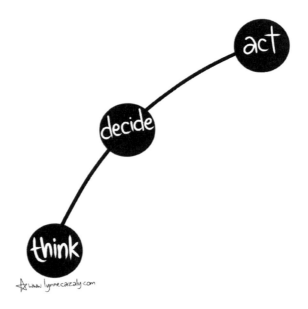

Sensemaking helps us understand the deeper meaning of what is going on. Sense-making. Making sense. While we are born with and grow to use some natural abilities in sensemaking, it's also a learnable skill. The better we are able to make sense of things, and the sooner we can, the better we can understand, decide and act.

Sensemaking tries to uncover, reveal, expose what lies beneath our thinking. It is about connecting the dots between seemingly unrelated things that do, in fact, make sense. There is a saying that we have, 'connecting the dots', to identify a trend or a theme. Our brains love to make sense. The act of sensemaking helps take messy, confusing or uncertain situations and events and … makes sense of them. Instead of feeling uncertain and confused, we feel calmer. As information makes sense, it becomes 'resolved' for us. We're less likely to lay awake at night pondering and problem solving if we've resolved things that were on our mind during the day.

Have you noticed yourself saying to people, 'Does that make sense?' or 'Oh, yes, that makes sense!' Have you heard people in conversation say, 'That doesn't make much sense,' or 'Brilliant, thank you, that makes total sense.'?

We are making sense constantly throughout the day, whether we are consciously aware of it or not. We are mentally connecting dots, joining threads, weaving, bringing different ideas, events and happenings together to resolve them satisfactorily in our minds.

connecting the dots

from lynnecazaly.com

In my book *Making Sense: A Handbook for the Future of Work* I researched several of the theories of sensemaking and put them together with practical skills, questions, templates and techniques to create a useful and practical guide. I wanted to make sense of sensemaking! It's such a brilliant human capability, and the better we can be at it, the better we will be at managing our life, who we are and what we do. And it is via this clever capability of sense-making that we can outsmart the Argh! of our overwhelm.

Why is making sense of our life useful?

Dr Robert Holden, in his book *Shift Happens*, said, 'every moment of your life you are deciding 1) who you are, 2) what you want, 3) what you can do, and 4) what you deserve and what you don't.'

This is directly linked to the sensemaking actions of thinking, deciding and acting. When we make sense of things, we feel more in control of them and more powerful to make decisions and take actions for ourselves and our life. Dr Holden explains that 'in effect, you're creating a self-image, an opinion of yourself'.

We are always sensemaking, about ourselves, about the world around us and our relationship to what's happening. What if we could do that in a way that made overwhelm easier to manage? How might we outsmart our overwhelm so we know how it works, how and why it happens and what to do instead?

Our seeking systems create the natural impulse to explore our worlds, learn about our environments and extract meaning from our circumstances.
– Daniel M Cable, Alive at Work

Our striving and at times struggle to understand what is going on is the hallmark of an uncertain and constantly changing world. As we try to do more and more, and juggle more and more, and have different roles, and deal with increasing technological demands, we can find ourselves overwhelmed with information and work. This crazy world we are in that is constantly changing gives us an opportunity to assess what is going on and to work out our relationship to it, and therefore what we should do about it.

These are the key questions of sensemaking:

What is going on?

and

What do I need to do about it?

☆ www.lynnecazaly.com

You will see those two questions come up frequently in this book.

As the world changes and things happen to us – whether they be good, bad or otherwise or we think of them to be so – we are trying to cope and live.

Often we struggle to cope because we don't make sense rapidly enough about what is going on. Many people are trapped in endless cycles of thinking and depressive thought. Others entertain thoughts of harm, and others are silently crying for some sort of support.

What if we could reduce the amount of overthinking we do, and if we could accelerate our decision making and action, remove the obstacles that get in our way, and increase our well-being? Do we think we could do this via medication? Or a meditation? Do we need to take up yoga? Eat healthier? Or just exercise a bit more?

What if the solution was better sensemaking? What if we asked better questions and explored what we were thinking and experiencing in overwhelm and then took action?

This would make our own lives better, and we would become better members of our families, communities, tribes and workplaces.

The bottom line is, that we need to live with ourselves. And live! Not suffer or struggle or deteriorate or close down. As the world increases in size, pressure and population, we need to create a greater number of independent thinkers who are willing to take control of their own lives and of the global issues that confront us.

Instead of feeling overwhelmed, what if we made sense?

The power of a sensemaking map

Where are you? And where are you going? We already enjoy a daily use of maps, looking at our phones or devices we might ask:

Where is my parcel delivery?
Why did the Uber driver go down that street?
Which is the quickest route to the park?

Maps have gone full circle (full globe?) from being crusty old, folded-the-wrong-way paper maps used on the National Lampoon's film series of family vacations, to books of maps, street directories and atlases, to apps of maps. We know what maps look like and use them all the time. They guide and show us the unknown, unseen.

So it's too bad (and so silly) that we don't use them ourselves. We don't need to wait for a cartographer to create maps for us; we can make our own. Yes! We can put pen to paper, marker to white board, stylus to tablet … in fact any writing tool to any writable surface and make ourselves a map.

We create hand drawn 'mud maps' which are rough sketches of locations to show people the way, point out landmarks and label streets and distances. When a group of friends were planning to gather at a farm one weekend for a social catch-up, the hand drawn sketch of where the farm was located was vital. The property wasn't on Google Maps so we needed that local knowledge of what was where to guide us. We drove along Millers Road for 3 kilometres, turned right at the Y intersection, past the second collection of mailboxes and then drove through the second black iron gate.

This was all on a map, hand drawn, roughly sketched, so we knew where we were going. And we all got there! No stress and definitely no overwhelm!

The maps we can use for better sensemaking can be similar in some ways to a street map or geographic atlas. We can use the same imagery, icons, words, shapes and lines that we would recognise on geographic maps. Maps show us roads, cities, train lines, oceans, parks and shops. Put together on a map, they help us make sense of where we are, what's around us and where we are going.

You may have heard of Tony Buzan's 'mind map' technique, where an idea is written in the centre of a page and thoughts are captured radiating out from the centre on little 'branches' or lines. This is just one type of map making. There is great potential for us to consider so many more kinds and types of maps ... depending on what's going on and what we need to do about it.

With a sensemaking map that we make for ourselves, we can connect our ideas, plot out information and gather our thoughts to make sense of where we are... and where we are going.

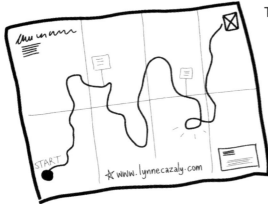

Thankfully, the father of sensemaking, Dr Karl Weick gives us permission to make any kind or quality of map when he says, 'any map will do.' It's the map that matters, that there is a map, not what it looks like or whether it's correct, perfect or even accurate.

The benefits of sensemaking

Making sense of what is going on brings us many benefits when we are overwhelmed:

- ☆ It helps us understand the story so far and some of the possible directions of what can happen next.

- ☆ It is a reflective activity which means we can look back on happenings to get a better perspective than when we are immersed in them.

- ☆ It helps us consider potential scenarios.

- ☆ It's useful for identifying the reality in a situation versus the unreality that the mind might be conjuring.

- ☆ It reveals patterns to us. Once we identify that the same thing keeps happening or a similar theme is emerging, it gives us power to decide to take different action.

- ☆ It helps us keep our eyes open and to continue to observe and make decisions.

- ☆ It gives us options and choices and empowers us with knowledge and know how.

- ☆ It helps us clarify and control our thoughts about what's going on and quickly see how things might be related.

- ☆ It can help us 'get out of our heads' and get our thoughts out of our overwhelmed mind.

- ☆ Most of all, sensemaking gives us rapid perspective. And when we are in a state of overwhelm, that is a mighty powerful place.

More than journaling

Sensemaking can take us further than journaling. Journaling – where we write in a diary or express our thoughts and feelings onto paper – has enjoyed an ongoing popularity, even in these digital times of living, looking at and learning via multiple screens. Moleskins and Leuchtturms and other bound notebooks are popular companions in satchels and handbags and on desks and bedside tables the world over. There's something empowering and resolving about getting our thoughts from 'in here' to 'out there'.

Kira M. Newman in 'How Journaling Can Help You in Hard Times' reminds us that while keeping a diary isn't new, writing – more effectively than over drawing alone – can help ease our stress when we're struggling.

The 'disclosing of emotions' rather than stuffing them down means, 'I'm able to organize thoughts and feelings on paper so they no longer take up room in my head,' explains Allison Quatrini, assistant professor at Eckerd College, quoted in Newman's article.

Quatrini further explains that 'writing forces us to organize our experiences into a sequence, giving us a chance to examine cause and effect and form a coherent story.'

Yes! This is sensemaking.

We get to 'put our experiences, thoughts, beliefs, and desires into language, and in doing so it helps us understand and grow and make sense of them,' adds Joshua Smyth, a professor of bio-behavioural health and medicine at Penn State University.

If we combine the benefits of a sensemaking map AND the powerful effects of journaling, we get a multiplied sensemaking skill that's got the power to deal with overwhelm. We will advance through it, up to the higher levels of the ladder shared earlier: out of drowning, struggling and juggling, and up to understanding, progressing and achieving.

Let's go there. Let's now make sense of our overwhelm, redefine our overwhelm from 'I'm so overwhelmed' to something more that we can think, understand and act on.

Part 1

The Load of Overwhelm

Introduction

Overwhelm isn't just one thing, once. It's a complex mix of loads and emotions that while vital for human functioning, can get out of our control or start running our life.

Understanding what overwhelm is and what it's made of will give us the power to redefine it, to not fall victim to its powerful vortex, and to instead be the master of our work, thoughts and emotions.

What is Overwhelm?

Dangerous storms have swept through South-East Freak Town overnight and into the morning, dumping heavy rain and causing flash flooding.

A weather agency said a shit-tonne heap of rain had fallen in the past four hours, more than three times the average for the month.

Weather forecasters have extended rain warnings up and down Crazy Country for the rest of the week, predicting the worst flooding in recent times.

These might be real (if adapted) flood warnings from media reporters and weather forecasters, but they can also remind us that weather comes and goes. It may deluge and flood, while at other times it can be arid and dry, and still others when it's just kind of ... normal.

In times of flood, we see people stacking sandbags to keep the rising waters at bay, there are road signs almost underwater and stock wandering to find higher ground. Vehicles can't get through where they would normally.

In times of drought, we see parched lands and dust bowls. And in times of normality, well, it's all kind of rolling along.

It's not just the earth that gets flooded. So do we! When we are 'flooded', we become overloaded and get overwhelmed. And the rest of the time, we're either 'dry', zoned out and unaffected, or we're just carrying on, normally.

In practical terms, overwhelm refers to the flow and inundation of water in times of flood. For us, overwhelm is a flood or inundation of work, information, emotions and thoughts about it all.

And the overwhelm experience is not the same for all of us.

It's as if we all have our own individual weather systems, delivering up a seasonal mix of floods, droughts and normal conditions as our life goes on, day by day.

In *The Age of Overwhelm*, author Laura van Dernoot Lipsky says, 'the state of overwhelm has many shades. It is a continuum ... experiencing some degree of overwhelm as a natural response to all that we encounter', is indeed, natural.

She continues, explaining that we might 'experience that as an occasional flutter of doubt, more frequent flooding of emotion, or ripping despair that we carry with us throughout our days.'

It's our own individual weather experience.

Some days are bright, sunny, fine. Other days might be dark and stormy, full of challenge, confusion and emotion. Still other days are neither. They're just … days.

As well as our own private weather system of overwhelm, there is a bigger global one that can impact us too.

Depending on what's going on in the world, our experiences of overwhelm can be affected. We can be influenced by what we see and experience in the world: from environmental concerns, political shake ups, social injustices, crimes and criminals, health problems, gender gaps and imbalances, social media impacts, family issues, power and control issues of imbalance or cruelty, social and community issues affecting our communities and every other thing occupying our view of the world from where we sit or stand.

Amy wondered, 'Is it just me? Is everyone else doing fine and it's only me? Or are we all somehow overwhelmed with something?'

Her new business coaching service was getting closer to going live and being launched into the world. And she was absolutely drowning in it, overwhelmed. There was a website and branding to finish, the online course structure and the resources for each topic to finalise, a client project report to edit, six blogs to write so her website had something on it, a payment gateway to choose so she could take payments from clients, and that wasn't all. There was the new calendar booking system and customer records system to get used to, social media posts to schedule, and her Wi-Fi was playing up, cutting in and out. If that wasn't enough, there was this dark foreboding cloud hanging around on the edges of her world, threatening to rain on her parade!

'I had this sense of "I'm going to lose my shit,"' was how Amy described it.

'I'm so loaded up with things to do, worries about the success, attention to the finer details and hopes for how it will work for my clients that I can't sleep at night!'

Well, she might fall asleep from exhaustion but then wakes wide-eyed at 3.17am with six more things buzzing around her head. Amy feels her heart pounding as her thoughts race ahead through the different pages of her website and whether the images do the program justice, whether people will understand what she's written and whether the payment gateway will accept foreign currency. She starts sweating, feels a tightness in her throat and a dread level of multi-million-dollar stock-exchange-listing Silicon Valley start-up proportions! 'I'm a solo business operator in a regional town!!', she groaned. 'Argh! Why does it have to be so *hard*?'

But do we classify overwhelm as being only 'good' or 'bad'? Perhaps it's not that extreme.

Amy was perhaps just as overwhelmed, but with different emotions, when she walked down the aisle with her now husband Dan. She was jittery, teary, 'laugh-crying, making noises a small puppy makes,' she recalls. 'I was so happy, so overjoyed! Come to think of it, I was overwhelmed then too. It was just different overwhelm'.

She was overwhelmed when she scored a job at a university; overwhelmed when she jumped out of a plane strapped on to a skydiving instructor; and she was overwhelmed when her girl-friends came over and cooked her dinner when she was recovering from the death of a close friend.

Overwhelm might show up as a leak or trickle at first, but then as the rains (emotions) continue and the tributaries (our body) collect all of that rain and transport it to our heart and mind, it's flood time, people! The waters rise and the emotions can feel like they're drowning us.

Many of the feelings of overwhelm can feel similar to the effects of life's big and little traumas. Accidents, disappointments, shocks, loss, grief, illness, natural disasters, separations, and conflict are some examples of how we experience trauma in our world.

As psychiatrist Dr Mark Epstein says in the *New York Times* article 'The Trauma of Being Alive', and in his book *Advice Not Given: A Guide to Getting Over Yourself*, 'trauma is not just the result of major disasters. It does not happen to only some people. An undercurrent of it runs through ordinary life'. He says that 'if we are not suffering from post-traumatic stress disorder, we are suffering from pre-traumatic stress disorder.'

Oh, what? Yes, our ordinary lives are far from ordinary or dull because they are surging and flooding with situations, fears, celebrations, experiences, worries and wonders that gather up our emotions and flood us with them. Regularly. Often. Are these a kind of 'minor' trauma that we experience? Repeatedly?

Just look at what's on our mind. If we take an inventory we'll see all of the thoughts that we are drowning under.

And where the heck is our dam wall, or at least some sandbags to hold back this imminent flood? Why are we so unprepared, even though this happens all the time? All. The. Time.

Perhaps we don't have sufficient sandbags to manage the arrival of overwhelm nor a dam and reservoir infrastructure to redirect and store the overwhelm when it inevitably reaches us.

Weather forecasters make predictions of what weather is coming by looking at the information available, scanning maps, data and radars. Could we make predictions of our own emotional forecast by considering our situation in the same way?

Yet, we can say 'yes' to a dozen things that will add to our to-do list and still act surprised when we fill up and experience over-whelm! We might behave like it's a surprise but perhaps there were warning signs all the way along.

Didn't we see it coming? Couldn't we read the signs? Or was it that we chose not to see them?

'I didn't see the speed limit sign, Officer.'

What were we doing? Who freaking knows, because we were overwhelmed after all! We weren't thinking clearly. Our attention can't possibly be working at 100% when we're already flooded and overwhelmed with all of that stuff, that stimuli that comes on into us and generates the flood of emotions.

Sometimes a tough conversation brings on a 'boom' of overwhelm. Overwhelm may not even announce its arrival, it's just ... there. One moment everything is all clear; the next it's inundation. The dam has broken and whole houses are floating by on the powerful flow and flood of overwhelm.

We might catastrophise, cry, get narky, angry, snippity, short and sharp, silent and scared, frustrated as the waters rise and our emotions bubble up.

With any heightened emotional experience, our bodies release stress hormones like adrenaline which prepare us for fight or flight. When we do neither but just keep pushing through, there is an excess of these hormones. Where do they go to? What do they do?

Like Amy, about to launch her business. She was waking up at 3am as a result of those adrenaline hormones, making her sweat and making her heart pound. The adrenaline lingers, taking perhaps hours to be dispersed and processed throughout and from our body. We stay flooded with reactive hormones that we didn't end up using, because we neither fought nor flew. Now there's a glut and an oversupply.

Our body generates still more hormones for anticipation, to prepare for what might happen. And as we mentally rehearse conversations or situations over and over, we drum up more reserves for more fighting or flighting.

A flood of emotions is released and then it's not used. No wonder Amy struggles to get back to sleep. Her body is ready for war! It's like after heavy rains where initial falls soak into the ground but then the ground is over-soaked and so water lies about.

We don't need to have overwhelm all the time. We can't. We'd die from exhaustion. So we must at some point manage to get through it and eat and sleep and post that parcel and buy some bananas and get the car serviced. We carry on and do the things of life without overwhelm freezing us.

If we have some natural way of moving on or through our overwhelm, eventually, how do we do that? And why don't we do it more often? How might we accelerate it or put it to work sooner so that overwhelm doesn't stay with us as long? How good would that be?

Ruth had to buy another car. Her previous one was no longer roadworthy after an accident repair didn't quite do the repair job well enough. Ruth thought of all of the things involved in buying a new car and she felt that as a single woman in her 50s, this was going to be filled with many overwhelming elements. Which car and from where? How much? What deal? Which to test drive? How to pick it up? Insurance? Extra features? Colour? Registration? Not to mention all of the admin and paperwork leftover from the transfer and sale of the damaged car. Added to this was the fact this happened during the early lockdowns of the COVID-19 pandemic, when just stepping out of the house was a big deal, let alone coordinating the purchase of a car. It wasn't buying four tomatoes from the supermarket or a coffee from her local cafe. It was a car, thousands of dollars' worth of car! It was a potentially overwhelming process.

Except it wasn't. Ruth sailed through each step, making decisions, doing the next thing and it all happened with little fuss, little challenge and few – if any – hiccups. Ruth could barely believe it.

With no overwhelm in sight for the entire process, Ruth was pleasantly surprised and uplifted by the experience. She floated above the experience, rather than being drowned in it. She was all over it. It wasn't all over her.

We all have tasks, responsibilities and projects that pass by without much of a fuss. Perhaps we don't notice them. We aren't overwhelmed when we do them. They don't overwhelm us. We carry on and we function. Why then do some things overwhelm us?

- Is it the quantity of work we have on?
- Is it the type of task we are doing?
- Is it the way we are tackling the task or project?
- Is it the emotions or meaning we have connected to the task?
- Is it the expectations we have?
- Is it the pressure we feel to do a good job?

The difference may be in the sense we make and the meaning we attach to events. You know, the classic psychological theory summarised by Shakespeare in Hamlet, that, 'there is nothing either good or bad, but thinking makes it so'.

What is this meaning we give events?

In the book *Forever Skills* by Kieran Flanagan and Dan Gregory, one of 'the 12 skills to future proof yourself, your team and your kids' is 'insight'. They say 'the ability to identify opportunities and make intelligent judgement has been, and always will be, critical.' They explain that one of ways to generate insight is to 'make meaning from the information you have gathered', and 'the meaning you create trumps raw numbers.'

It's often how we think about what we are doing – or want or hope to do – that brings the rains and floods of overwhelm. If we didn't care about it, we may be more objective, just do the task and then it would be done. It's 'no big deal'.

Then the times when it is a 'big deal', what's going on? Why is it a big deal?

If we can identify and understand the meaning we attach to events and occurrences, expectations and goals, we will make great progress towards understanding our own weather system of overwhelm: preparing for what's forecast, responding to whatever happens, and feeling capable, even when we're not sure what's ahead.

Those sensemaking questions, right? What's going on? What do I need to do about it?

While purchasing a car wasn't as overwhelming as Ruth expected, finalising her will was. The decision of who would receive her estate when she died held big meaning for her. Siblings, nieces, nephews and dear friends. What would she do? It reminded her of her parents' deaths and the assets that were entrusted to her in the family name. Maybe this was why the will was such a sticking point for her and an overwhelming experience every time she got 'the folder' off the shelf.

For our overwhelm, it's all about the meaning we give things. If we can make sense of what's going on, we can decide what to do about it. And then do it.

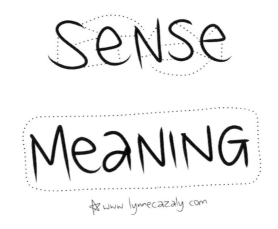

What's the payoff?

Staying in overwhelm and not resolving it does something for us.

It gives us some kind of 'pay off' or reward.

Psychologists know that we get hooked into our own behaviour patterns because they do something for us. Most of all, these patterns are EASY to follow! Susan McQuillan, in *Psychology Today*, explains that 'no matter how early you started [a habit], you weren't born doing any of them. You *learned* how to do them. Learned behaviour is a wonderful thing because it makes life so much easier.' And with habitual behaviours, we know that we 'do them without even thinking.'

'But learned behaviour,' she explains 'that allows you to act without thinking is not such a good thing when it results in bad habits that become difficult … to break.'

If overwhelm is one of our habitual responses, might it serve us to break the habit?

What do you imagine the deeper payoffs or returns are to us if we get overwhelmed … and stay there?

Of course, some overwhelm is a natural part of survival, to see what is important to us or what might endanger us or to prompt us to change how we are thinking and behaving. But why else?

Perhaps like personal training and fitness, as we put the body under stress, it is able to cope with more. Do we build a tolerance to pressure? If we've juggled and struggled with our daily lives, do we cope better when the big stuff of life happens, like deaths, accidents, loss, grief, growth?

Might we fall into some patterns of our preferred ways of coping? Stephen B. Karpmann's 'drama triangle' comes to mind. While it's a model about human interaction and conflict, do we play one of the three roles in the triangle by staying in overwhelm? Which of the three roles might link best to overwhelm?

There is:

> The persecutor, or 'it's all your fault!'
> The rescuer, or 'let me help you.'
> The victim, or 'poor me.'

This fascinating playing out of roles in conflict happens because we take a position, and we often do it unconsciously.

Let's zoom in on the persecutor role. Do we say, 'It's your fault that I've got so much on! You make me do this job; you're the bad guy here!'

How about the rescuer: 'Here, let me take on that load for you. I'll do that, to save you. Let me help, I'll do it.'

And then zoom in on the victim role. What happens when we say or think, 'Poor me; I'm so overwhelmed.'? What is it *really* saying?

Is it saying:

> *Give me a hand.*
> *You should really help out.*
> *There's so much to do.*
> *I'm the only one that works around here.*
> *Look after me because I've been really working hard.*
> *I've got a lot on my plate.*
> *I'm so busy.*
> *There's too much on.*

These kinds of thoughts could be a reason why we seek a state of overwhelm and stay in it. Perhaps we get something from other people when we are busy, overwhelmed or overloaded. Perhaps we get to rescue them, or they get to rescue us, pay us more attention, or support us more. Maybe we have to reach overwhelm before they'll notice we're here.

Stress and time management author Peter Bregman says in *Four Seconds*, 'our reaction to feeling stressed about how much work we have is often competitive complaining'.

If I've got more on my plate than you, does that mean I'm better, work harder and am a more valuable or useful member of society? Does it mean I deserve more attention, sympathy and support? Do I believe I should share in greater rewards because I'm doing it tough?

A mentor early in my career had a pivotal conversation with me at one of our monthly meetings. I'd said I was 'so busy' and 'so overwhelmed', and she advised me wisely that 'awards aren't given for martyrdom; progress isn't made easier with suffering.'

A *Healthline* article suggests that, historically, a martyr 'is someone who chooses to sacrifice their life or face pain and suffering instead of giving up something they hold sacred ... Today, the term is sometimes used to describe someone who seems to always be suffering in one way or another.'

Do we ever find ourselves in overwhelm because it is our suffering that people might notice?

While it might feel good to have some of that love and attention, sympathy and care for a short while because we are 'so busy', it ends up spiralling us – and others – into a negative and less helpful space. Perhaps it's an addictive feeling and we want more of it.

What's the PAYOFF?

www.lynnecazaly.com

Does this sound like some of the conversations you have?

– *'How are you?'*

    – *'I've been soooooo busy. How about you?'*

– *'Oh yes, I've got sooooooo much on'.*

    – *'Well, I've got so much to do that I didn't even have time to eat lunch!'*

– *'I've got so much on that I've worked 60 hours this week!'*

… and on the competitive complaining goes.

Ponder it … are there benefits that you gain by being overwhelmed or staying overwhelmed? And do we engage in competitive complaining about the state of our overwhelm in an effort to get something else?

The Loads We Carry

When we're overwhelmed, we're often overloaded … or have been overloaded, recently.

There are three main loads we carry:

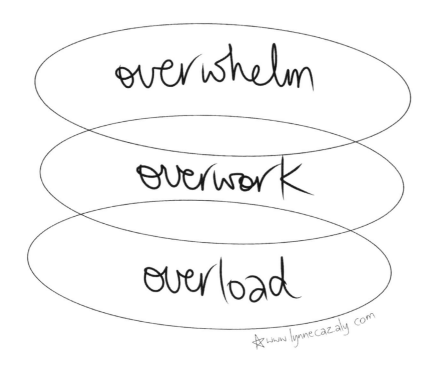

overwhelm

overwork

overload

☆www.lynnecazaly.com

The load of overwhelm – when it happens ... sometimes it sneaks up on us; an unpleasant surprise. There is an emotional load here – sometimes called 'emotional labour' – it's the emotional response and load of our actions. The emotional load of overwhelm could be stress and anxiety, worry and concern, fear or agitation, or we could be feeling a flood of joy, love, gratitude and excitement.

The load of work – these are the physical and mental tasks we carry out. Whether we are a project manager, home and family manager, team manager or just managing our own life, there is a load of 'stuff' we have to do. Understanding how we do it and how else we can do it helps us work with this load and prevent it from becoming an even more overwhelming load.

The load of information – this is the never-ending flow of information that's ours to devour or disappear under. We can buckle under the load of information we receive daily ... or hourly if you've been on back-to-back Zoom calls! How do we handle information – whether we are reading it, trying to learn it and 'get our head around it', scanning over it quickly, speaking it with others, meeting people about it or struggling to understand it?

Rather than let overwhelm overwhelm us, we can take control. And not in a 'control freak' way but in a smart, clever, confident and capable way.

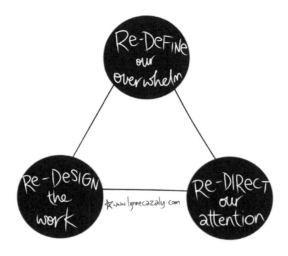

If we can do these three things …

1. re-define the overwhelm (Part 1)

2. re-imagine the work (Part 2), and

3. re-direct our attention (Part 3)

… we will understand, act on and ultimately outsmart our overwhelm.

Why We Get Overwhelmed

There are many reasons why we get overwhelmed and discovering why or making sense of it is part of outsmarting it.

If we don't manage the loads we have, we can easily become overwhelmed.

Did we see the additional work coming but took it on and said 'yes' to it anyway?

Did we ignore it and it was just automatically added to our 'to do' list?

Did we create the burden ourselves – perhaps without realising it – taking on additional tasks, roles and responsibilities?

It can look like this:

www.lynnecazaly.com

Some of the ways we get overwhelmed include:

⭐ Lack of help available or offered; perhaps we're alone in this project, task or situation.

⭐ Making up for lost time; are we trying to move faster, accelerate our project or tasks to 'catch up' on lost or missed opportunities, previous delays or time wasted?

⭐ The pressures and expectations of gender bias, discrimination, and other societal inequities.

⭐ Believing that doing more or working harder will create a better result or lead to sooner or better success.

- If we don't do more we might be seen as incapable or less capable.

- It's so freaking competitive in the world right now; if we don't go hard, we could lose out and fall behind.

- We think we 'should' or believe it's just what you do and it's how life is.

- Fear or inability to say 'no' or not comply with a request.

- We don't know that there are alternative ways of outsmarting overwhelm.

Spiralling into overwhelm

What comes first do you think? Do we get overloaded with work to do and then feel overwhelmed? Or do we experience an overload of information and then feel the overwhelm? Or do we just cut to the chase and experience overwhelm?

I believe we experience loads of loads. That is, we get loaded with work, loaded with information and loaded with emotion. And that's human and most likely, manageable. But then when we don't deal with these – when we don't 'unload' – we end up carrying it all around with us, in us. As more work, information and emotion piles on, hour after hour or day after day, we reach a limit of overload.

And we may be able to carry on for a while, juggling, struggling, drowning ... until it's too much and we experience overwhelm.

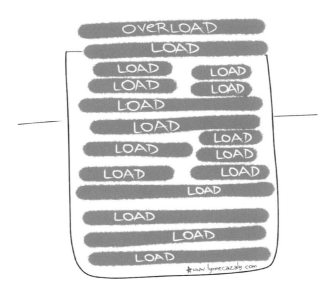

We push on and persist through overload and overwhelm when perhaps we should pause.

—

Sensemaking the Overwhelm

Overwhelm: the word is so often used as a catch-all, a general term to describe a state we are in, something we are experiencing or our reaction and response.

It's not fair to make one word do all that work! Nor does it pick up on the nuances and individuality of us. We know that our overwhelm can be different to other people's.

Let's redefine what overwhelm actually is. And perhaps this is the thing: we're using a single word that can have some extreme meanings to label some of the experiences, emotions and situations we have.

How might we understand and explain this better? What does overwhelm really mean? How do we explain it better so we're not rushing to elevate, exaggerate or extreme-ise what's going on for us, but more accurately explain what's going on? Some examples:

EXAMPLE 1. Earlier this week I was an attendee (in listen-only mode!) on a webinar. It was 90 brilliant minutes of great content; information and ideas flowing fast. I couldn't pause it – it was live! And before long, I was racing, trying to catch the key points, take notes, listen and multi-task my way through it. Argh! I was overwhelmed. Or was I?

EXAMPLE 2. Yesterday watching the news on TV, there was story after story of sadness, drama, crime and misery. After 20 minutes, it was too much for me. Tears welled in my eyes, worst-case scenarios came into my mind and I just wanted to hide. Argh! I was overwhelmed. Or was I?

EXAMPLE 3. This morning before an early meeting at 7.30am, I was trying to get my breakfast ready; toast, yoghurt, fruit, cold water, lemon, hot milk for a cup of chai tea … so many things to get ready at the same time and to get online to the meeting with the sometimes-tricky Microsoft Teams app. It was all too much. Argh! I was overwhelmed. Or was I?

In each of these examples, my default response was, 'I'm overwhelmed! Argh!' But on closer inspection, I realised that for each of them:

1. I was overloaded. I had information overload, after concentrating for quite a while, plus a bit of excitement about these wonderful ideas and possibilities!

2. I was having an emotional response to the (often over-dramatised) reporting of world events in the news media.

3. I was rushing and multi-tasking my way towards a deadline … and I was a bit hungry too! Hangry perhaps?

With some greater reflection and understanding, I could see that each of these situations had a cause or lead-up to the overwhelm.

It is often during the most challenging times where there is the greatest opportunity to redefine yourself.
— Dr Shilagh Mirgain

At our most overwhelmed moments, might we be able to redefine the overwhelm?

Emotions of overwhelm

On top of our overload can be a layer or four of emotions! Often referred to as 'emotional labour', it's the emotional effort or consequences of what we're thinking or doing. It almost always accompanies the load of work AND the load of information, yet we don't often think about it or make sense of it.

In the article 'You're doing emotional labor, whether you realise it or not', author Joe Deer remarks that 'feelings are hard work' and that living through a pandemic in 2020 and beyond has shown many people that. First defined by Arlie Russell Hochschild back in the 1980s, emotional labour 'requires' us to induce or suppress feeling so we can do what we need to do. And we don't just work on our own emotions; we work hard to kind of manage and influence the emotions of others.

Many industries call on a high need for emotional labour. Think of healthcare workers, teachers, therapists, customer-facing workers.

How does a surgeon show up and focus when they've just had a distressing argument with a family member? How does a customer service team member feel empathy for a client's situation when their own cat has died? How does a workplace trainer keep focused on the group's needs after receiving some critical health information on the phone? As Deer remarks, 'when we step back and look at it, it's clear that we're all doing emotional labor. We do it instinctively and may not even realize it's happening.'

To ignore the emotional side of work, the emotional labour, is to risk burn-out. It's not that we need to stop every moment to 'check our feels'.

But as Deer says, 'just by being aware that emotional labour exists, you're better able to recognize it.' Then we can make sense of it, understand it and work with it rather than against it. It's a kind of adaptability, flexibility or agility.

Dr Susan David's book *Emotional Agility* is a great insight to understanding more about how our emotions work and how they can contribute to our overwhelm. This doesn't mean we don't need our emotions! We're not trying to outsmart them alone, it's the whole overload, overload, overload and then overwhelm that we can outsmart. So understanding emotions and recognising them as an important part of being a human is healthy stuff.

To redefine our generically labelled overwhelm – and the emotional overwhelm that can rise – take a wander through this list of emotions from Dr Susan David. Rather than 'overwhelmed', is there one, two or three – or 15! – here that make greater sense to you?

A List of Emotions

Go beyond the obvious to identify exactly what you're feeling.

Angry	Sad	Anxious	Hurt	Embarrassed	Happy
Grumpy	Disappointed	Afraid	Jealous	Isolated	Thankful
Frustrated	Mournful	Stressed	Betrayed	Self-conscious	Trusting
Annoyed	Regretful	Vulnerable	Isolated	Lonely	Comfortable
Defensive	Depressed	Confused	Shocked	Inferior	Content
Spiteful	Paralyzed	Bewildered	Deprived	Guilty	Excited
Impatient	Pessimistic	Sceptical	Victimized	Ashamed	Relaxed
Disgusted	Tearful	Worried	Aggrieved	Repugnant	Relieved
Offended	Dismayed	Cautious	Tormented	Pathetic	Elated
Irritated	Disillusioned	Nervous	Abandoned	Confused	Confident

Source: Dr Susan David

Re-defining our overwhelm is a highly powerful technique to control how we are impacted by it. And it's a key step in the process of outsmarting it.

1. Pause

Stop everything for a moment. You don't need to stop it forever, just lift your head up, stand up from your desk, put down the tools you're using, walk out of the space or situation you're in.

Get some clear air and some perspective.

Look at what's happening.

2. Locate

Locate yourself on the Ladder of Overwhelm. Are you somewhere you'd rather not be?

Note some of the things you're experiencing. If you're in the bottom half, what are you drowning under? What are you struggling with? What are you juggling?

3. Re-Label

Rethink the overwhelm — what is it really?

Switch on your sensemaking and ask those two questions:

Rather than thinking more and more, try this sense map and get the information and thinking out of your head. Put the name, title, or key word about your project, task or challenge in the middle, or write the emotions or experiences you're having. In the segments, list the things that are on your mind. What's there ...?

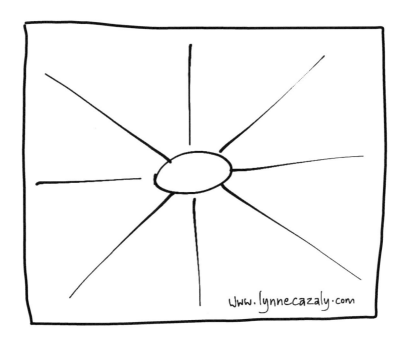

www.lynnecazaly.com

Use this tool to make deeper sense of what's going on.

What happened	I felt	It was really
I was listening on a webinar, to 90 minutes of content and it was brilliant. Information and ideas were flowing fast and I couldn't pause it because it was live. Then I was racing trying to catch the key points and take notes and listen and multi-task and ... Argh !!!	Overwhelmed	I had information overload after concentrating for quite a while plus a bit of excitement about all of these ideas and possibilities.

On this 'map' we ask:

What happened?
I felt …
It was really …

This tool has helped me get a handle on overwhelm on many, many occasions and to see what's really going on. I get some perspective on the things contributing to my overwhelm.

Redefining our overwhelm is a great technique for being the boss of and outsmarting overwhelm. We get to swiftly redefine it and call the experience and our response what it is.

You'll see how sensemaking starts to become this deliberate skill of life, for life. To help us understand what's going on … and what we can or need to do about it.

Nothing in life is to be feared, it is only to be understood. Now is the time to understand more, so that we may fear less.
– Marie Curie

Download these templates and other resources at
www.lynnecazaly.com.au/argh

Summary

1. **Acknowledge that overwhelm is a flood of emotions** … and likely occurs after a period of time when you've been overloaded. We all experience it at varying times and in varying degrees.

2. **Name and redefine overwhelm.** Rather than saying, 'I'm so overwhelmed,' all the time, say it for what it really is. 'I'm frustrated; I've got six things on my to-do list to finish before 4pm and my teammates are standing around chatting and not helping out,' or 'I'm nervous; I've got to pick up the catering and decorations for Lydia's party and don't want to disappoint her,' or 'I'm feeling tearful; that is such a sad story to hear. It hurts my heart.'

3. **Make greater meaning of what's going on.** Stop for a moment and think about why a particular task or project is so important to you. Why is it emotional? Why do you think it needs to be done in a certain way?

4. **Notice the patterns.** Are there certain events, activities or triggers you have that act like a rain dance? Are there times when you 'just know' what's going to happen?

5. **Remember that not all overwhelm is alike – within us, or among us.** What happened before may be different in the future; how they handled or responded is different to how we might respond.

As we reach the end of this first part of the book, The Load of Overwhelm, we've looked at:

☆ what overwhelm means

☆ the emotions we might label as overwhelm

☆ where we can be on the Ladder of Overwhelm

☆ how we can redefine overwhelm so that it makes greater meaning for us.

Here's a map…

the OVERWHELM	❶ PAUSE	❷ LOCATE	❸ RELABEL
	Re-define the overwhelm		
			☆www.lynnecazaly.com

Let's now explore one of the main things that overloads us and leads us towards overwhelm … the load of work.

Part 2

The Load of Work

Introduction

Work. Load. Argh! It already feels heavy. When is it ever 'light', anyway? The fact it is referred to as a workload says there is a weight to carry, a burden to crumble under or a list of tasks pages and pages long to be done. Oh, the load!

The load we carry is like a ship or truck carrying freight and cargo. Surely, we delicate humans aren't meant to carry a LOAD?

Whatever 'work' is for you, it's vital to recognise the load that working – and overworking – can contribute to our experiences of overload and ... overwhelm.

Invisible Work
(Visualise the work)

On a recent visit to my local office supplies store, I was keen to just browse through what's new, but it was soon clear that the productivity industry was trying to tell me something. Or sell me something!

It's a hard sell. They've got targets to meet, sales to achieve and product to shift. It's a marketing machine.

Products like planners and diaries and post-its and journals and boxes and note pads and binders and so many kinds of tools – sticky-marker-poster-tape-folders ... all with a promise to fix our perceived productivity problems.

Unfortunately, they try and make us think we:

- ☆ are disorganised
- ☆ don't achieve anything
- ☆ need their product to remove our pain of overwhelm.

It's not true!

It's the same with new apps, other new products and services, promising to increase our productivity.

'Buy more stuff!' to get in control of all that you've already got. And each tool or solution tries to be the silver bullet to our disorganisation.

But now that we know more about overwhelm, it would be crazy to think one special kind of wall planner or one productivity app will resolve the challenges of overwhelm.

It's more likely to add to it – because we have to buy it, learn it, not use it, shame ourselves for not using it 'properly' and then the overwhelm continues … perhaps worse than before! And we return to the stationery store to search for another product or scan the app store for another app to solve the overload.

ENOUGH, I say!

One single thing won't help us get all over our overwhelm, but several things working together – that WORK FOR US – will.

The thing to beware of is that working – whatever work is for you – and overworking can contribute to our overload and over-whelm. And this work is likely part of our deeper, instinctive drives, so says social researcher and author Hugh Mackay. In *What Makes Us Tick?* he presents the 'ten desires that drive us' and some of them that include a nod to workload include:

- ☆ the desire to be taken seriously

- ☆ the desire to be useful

- ☆ the desire for more

- ☆ the desire for control.

How can we satisfy these desires and still not fall victim to the dangers of overload and overwork?

Whatever 'work' is for you

Our load of 'work' ranges from shopping for food, digging out tax file numbers, weeding the garden, taking out the trash, tasks and chores to complete, admin to finish, homework to supervise, paperwork to fill out, bills to pay, claims to complete. And that doesn't even begin to include the load we're given in a job role by bosses, bosses' bosses and our clients, customers, peers and colleagues.

The nature of what is work is changing and the definition or description of it is shifting. What may have been only paid work, now extends to work at home, work in our community, work at the kids' school, work with a sports team or recreational interest, work to keep a circle of friends connected and socialising, and work to just keep our life, home and family running.

And is everyone trying to offload their load onto someone else's load, or what?

If we could just get someone else to pick up some of our load: to cook our dinner, clean the bathroom, get the car serviced, do the homework, finish the laundry, tidy the desk, plan the holiday, book the doctor's appointments, get the remote fixed, get a new battery for the other remote, empty the bin, clean the table … and on and on it goes.

This doesn't even include the fun stuff, like reading, listening to music, catching up on the latest episode of <insert your favourite Netflix viewing> or walking/washing/feeding the furry creatures you might live with.

Our workload today includes plenty more than paid work and life's general chores and tasks. The gendered division of labour 'shows a persistent pattern of women doing a lot more housework and childcare than men', according to a study from 2019. The research, based on interviews with around 8500 opposite sex couples, found:

- ☆ 'Women do 16 hours of household chores every week, men do closer to six.

- ☆ Women did the bulk of the domestic chores in 93% of couples.

- ☆ There was a 50-50 split of domestic chores in 6% of couples.

- ☆ Only 1% of couples had men doing more domestic work than women.'[1]

The research by McMunn, Bird, Webb and Sacker from University College London and published in the journal *Work, Employment and Society* confirms the additional burden that many women carry before we even start talking about a paid job role.

This is recognition of a significant workload that's being carried ... often by one person.

Is that person you?

The load from the self

Among all of those things we load onto our 'to do' and 'to be' lists, is the load from ourselves. There are many things we're placing on that list that other people may not

- ☆ ask us to do

- ☆ expect us to do

- ☆ or even notice if we didn't do them.

So, why do we keep doing them?

Sure, sure, the rubbish bin overflowing or the empty fridge or pantry might cause a revolt or at least some whining, the cat would get annoyed and a friend might be disappointed but how often do we consider **what** is on our load and **how** the heck it got there?

No trucking company would transport something from Point A to Point B without knowing who ordered it, who is dispatching it, and its estimated weight and value, at a minimum. But there we go accepting – and VOLUNTEERING, offering and saying, 'Yes, I'll do it, pick me,' – to add plenty of work to our workload, because ... well, because!

The expectations we have for what needs to be done, should be done and ought to be done is often coined in the 'coulda woulda shoulda' phrasing.

> I **coulda** done better if I'd had more time.
> I **woulda** collected you from the airport.
> I **shoulda** baked a cake for their birthday.

Whether we express these expectations outwardly or simply have an internal conversation about it, our expectations show us what we would have liked to have done or hoped to have done. It's a peek into a box of dashed hopes we were likely trying to load onto our already overloaded load!

Seth Godin, marketing guru, published author and all-round clever thinker, speaks plenty of truth on this topic. His daily posts – which he's committed to writing and sharing every day for over 10 years – says: 'An overloaded truck isn't a more efficient way to move gravel (or anything else).'

No truck can take on more load if it is already full. It's such a powerful metaphor. There is only so much physical space in that truck – and legal space too, if you adhere to the weight rules of a fully-laden vehicle.

The truck can't take anymore ... until its emptied.

You can have your pebbles, sand or plants delivered from a landscape gardener on a truck, only once the truck is emptied from the previous delivery job. It makes logical sense and we can see the truck is full. Yet when it comes to our own load, we expect we can take on more and more and still more ... never emptying our original load. What the truck?!

What are these expectations?

Expectations are 'strong beliefs that something will happen or be the case', so says the Oxford Languages Dictionary.

It's an assumption we make, a kind of prediction or crystal balling ahead of time. We set a standard or raise a bar and believe that things will reach that height, hit that mark and fall into place.

And then it doesn't.

And we can be overwhelmed by that.

Overwhelm shows up in the load we take on, adding more to our already full truck.

Overwhelm continues to show up when things don't go the way we were expecting.

That flood of emotion from disappointment of dashed hopes combines with the initial overwhelm we felt from the quantity, size and amount of load we're carrying. Now we've got an overwhelming load, plus an overwhelming disappointment about how we can't carry any more or 'enough' load.

Much of this is tied to expectations. These are the tiny, multiple agreements or commitments we make with ourselves. Silently. They are the micro-hopes we have of what we'd like to make happen, get done or see through. And on a daily basis we're lumping more and more of these agreements, commitments and promises onto our truck.

Breakdown ahead! Overloaded trucks can't keep going. Neither can we.

What about their expectations?

What if our expectations are in check but it's THEM?

The expectations of others add a further load to our workload and in turn, adds to the potential overwhelm we can experience.

Can we get it done to their expectations? Will it be good enough? What if it's not? What will they think? They'll think I'm hopeless and can't bake a thing, that I can't even make a stupid salad!

In the article 'Perfectionism Is Increasing and That's Not Good News' in the *Harvard Business Review*, perfectionist researchers Thomas Curran and Andrew P. Hill found that it is the expectations from others that are driving the increase in many of us to pursue higher standards. We THINK 'they' – whoever they be – will want it a certain way. We KNOW they will be unbearable if it's not the way they want it. We BELIEVE other people have high standards and we THINK we have to reach them or do better than them, exceed them.

Here are those pesky expectations again. According to that research, these expectations are most often built on PERCEPTION, or 'how things seem'. It may not be accurate or true … although it can certainly feel true!

The weight and power of an expectation – whether ours or someone else's – is a load indeed. No wonder our truck feels full, even if there's not much physical work to do, we may be carrying an invisible load of 12 boxes, 3 pallets and 6 rolls of expectations about how things should be.

High expectations set in one area of our life rarely stay in that part of our life. It's more likely these expectations are across many parts of life.

And so our 'to do' list is full and overflowing with projects, tasks, commitments, expectations, beliefs and plenty of 'shoulds' to be ticked off. It's no wonder we never reach the end of a list; there is always, always more than could be done.

This happened to a colleague who could barely enjoy her wedding day because of the endless hours, late nights and extra work she'd put in to 'make it perfect'. There was so much extra load she'd been carrying for weeks – and months – that on the day of the ceremony and reception, she was exhausted and couldn't really enjoy it. Add to that the emotional overwhelm of seeing friends and family from overseas and it was a day of constant overwhelm. She said, 'I couldn't really enjoy it because I was so exhausted!'

Our workload will always be present in our life, unless we suddenly become a superstar celebrity who can delegate every little task out to a paid staff member! If we will always have a load, it is worth us understanding what we're carrying, why we're carrying it and if it really is 'paying its way' or just freeloading a ride with us.

Externalise the workload

Could a cause of our overwhelm be that we simply have too much 'on our minds'?

Do we keep mental notes and checklists, mental images of scenarios, and mental files of ideas and 'must do' items? All inside our head?

The task of writing down what we're thinking about is a powerful mental wellbeing tool, and we can use it for productivity, peace of mind and to outsmart our overwhelm too.

Write it all down

When overwhelm hits, strikes or sneaks up, there is a fairly well-known technique we can apply: write it all down. It's like the spoke template in Part 1. Whether the overwhelm flood strikes at 3am or 9.30am or 4pm, get the overwhelm out of your head. We need to do something with it, otherwise it continues to cycle and spin around. Problems get worse in our mind; tasks seem to multiply like rabbits; the urgency of our 'to do' list seems to accelerate. To write it all down is to externalise the information — to get it out of our mind.

While many people know of this technique, fewer try it, and still fewer use it as a coping and sensemaking method. Why would that be? 'I've heard of that,' or 'yeah, I know that,' is a response to a known solution, but if we track further, we might find the application of the method is missing. I know it, but I don't do it. I know I should probably lift weights, but I don't do it. I know I should turn off my screen before bedtime, but I don't do it. So the perception then is, 'this task will be hard.' How DO I write down everything in my head? What if this task never ends … I've got a lot in my head you know! What if I don't like what I see? What if the contents of my head aren't pretty?

Aha, and this is the premise of sensemaking. The creation of a map. The making visible what is invisible. And it is many of these invisible things that add to overwhelm purely because we CAN'T see them. If we do make them visible, even as a line of text, or some words encircled or a phrase in a box, it is out of our over-whelmed mind and into an external source. The actual overwhelm becomes visible, the feelings subside and the mind comes back to a balance. The flood is held at bay; the water is bailed out; the plug is removed and the overwhelm drains away.

Do it now … I'll wait here. Get a piece of paper, a notebook and pen and get ready to write – rather than type on a digital device – and write down what's on your mind, what you're working on, what you've got to do.

Why handwriting? It's been shown to create greater brain activity, and is associated with better thought organisation and an increased ability to generate ideas, according to 'Keyboards Are Overrated. Cursive is Back and it's Making Us Smarter'. That's a win, win, and another win!

So what to do with all of these things from our mind that are now written down?

The answer isn't a to-do list

Most of us are familiar with to-do lists and how they can be long, endless, detailed things that never seem to be … done.

The bad news about to-do lists gets broken to us in the *Harvard Business Review* article 'To-Do Lists Don't Work' by Daniel Markovitz.

The five problems with them are:

1. There's too much choice – because we can only handle up to about seven items or options before we're overwhelmed.

2. Too many big, complex tasks – the joy of crossing an item off the list can take a long time!

3. Too many different priorities – when they're all mixed up in the same list it can be difficult to sort them or make sense of them and completing all of the 'A' rated priorities and letting the 'C' priorities slip on by.

4. Lack of context – a short phrase of just a few words about a task just doesn't give us enough information, including the vitally important, how long will it take?

5. All list, no commitment – the lists don't help us make or build commitment to actually doing or completing the tasks.

So, if to-do lists aren't so effective, what do we do or use instead?

Visualise the work to be done

Even if we find to-do lists useful for capturing the number of things to do, the list falls short because we tend to write just the task; and nothing more detailed about it, when the deadline is or how long we think we might need to get it done.

Modern productivity tools like diaries, notes apps, reminders, timers, calendars, planners and noticeboards all have a place in our world. And they are all capable of reducing our overwhelm. While there is no 'one right way' to use them, there is the opportunity to find a way that works for us. And we may need to experiment a little with that.

The to-do list can be evolved and improved and I'd love to share with you the visualised to-do list that works a treat. So where is your current list? Is it on your mobile phone or device, in an app? Or is it in a notepad or paper diary?

Have you ever used a to-do list that's on the wall?

Kanban as a visual management tool

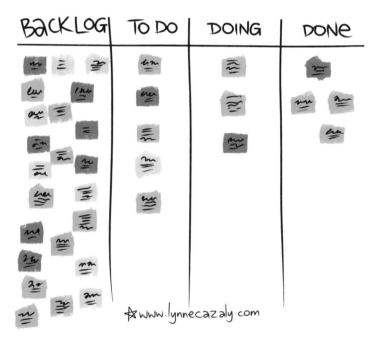

'Kanban' is a Japanese word for 'sign board'. The technique of Kanban – which originated via the lean manufacturing processes of the Toyota Production System – focuses on managing work by balancing demands and available capacity. It helps reduce bottle-necks and gives users of the technique the option of 'pulling' work when capacity permits, rather than work being 'pushed' through whether we have the availability to do it or not.

In the work I've done with software developers and agile project teams over the past 10 years, it's Kanban that I would label as one of the best ways to manage work load.

Kanban 'provides context for work, allowing us to go beyond mere productivity and experience greater efficiency and real effectiveness,' says Jim Benson and Tonianne DeMaria Barry in the brilliant book *Personal Kanban: Mapping Work, Navigating Life*.

Aha, there's a reference to maps and mapping again! There's a common theme here, hey? Most of all, Kanban is a productivity tool that helps limit the work we are doing yet somehow it helps us accomplish more.

We work out what we have to do, don't do too much of it at once, and do the most important task. It helps reduce the potential for overwhelm by managing the load we are carrying. And the 'sign board' part of Kanban recommends visualising – on a wall or in a specifically designed app – a kind of map of your work.

Kanban is a more evolved version of a to-do list and productivity system. It often has several columns, not one big 'to do'. I like using four columns, labelled:

- ☆ Backlog (what might be a traditional to-do list)
- ☆ To do (the work that is almost ready to start working on)

☆ Doing (the three tasks I'm currently working on – yes, I limit it to three. More on that is coming in the next chapter. Stay tuned!)

☆ Done (the tasks I've recently completed).

Is Kanban new for you? It's worth knowing about it as a way to not only SEE what you've got on, but also MANAGE and PROGRESS through it all. I can't speak highly enough or recommend Kanban highly enough. I've used it to write books, run projects, and I use it daily. Every single day.

Overwhelmed by scale or size of the work

When the gap is too big between where we are and where we'd like to be, it can seem insurmountable, uncrossable, impossible.

It's a huge step towards a big goal. After all, we've been told to 'dream big' haven't we?

While we know every journey begins with a single step, it can look more like a leap or pole vault from where we are. The gap may be too big for us to imagine crossing or closing.

And then … 'Oh hello overwhelm, you cheeky beast!'

The reality is, the perceived size of a project, task or piece of work is often what overwhelms us. We haven't considered all of the slices but we know it's a big job.

And so, BOOM, we try and manage all of that in our mind at once.

If the work or task is too big to manage, handle or imagine, there is potential for us to be overwhelmed.

Big task workers like those in the building and construction industry know that slicing work down into smaller sizes is effective. To try and build a whole building, or a whole house or whole skyscraper in one step would be overwhelming, not to mention impossible!

Project managers know that breaking things down is the secret to getting them done.

Landscape gardeners know it too.

Health practitioners treating a disease or illness know it.

Personal trainers, airline pilots, and explorers all know it too.

The work to be done cannot be done in one BIG step, but in many smaller steps.

The thinner the slice or smaller the step, the less overwhelming it is, and the more likely it can be done in the time we can make available.

Breaking a task down into manageable chunks isn't new advice. The 'how to eat an elephant' meme is out there … and the answer is 'one bite at a time'.

And despite us knowing this, we still embark on projects and chunks of work that are too big.

There's a reason why recipes are broken down into steps; it's so we can follow them, tick off the steps and get the thing done, and it works.

There's a reason why athletes train, showing up every day on the path to the elite success they dream of; one race won't do it for them – they'll need to break their goal down into a lot of other smaller steps of achievement.

I discovered this so plainly when I wrote my first book, *Visual Mojo*. Thinking that I have to sit down and 'write my book' is too big a task, too big a bite to try and take. All the writing that needs to be done … thousands of words … it's overwhelming!

But once I broke it down and made the project elements thinner, sliced it thinner, it was easier to see the possibilities of getting it done, and the realities of getting it done. I broke it down in to things like:

- ☆ deciding on the title

- ☆ cover design brief for the designer

- ☆ initial structure of 10 chapters

- ☆ key research papers to reference

… and so on. These were doable.

Start slicing. Take a big task that's on your to-do list, that is overwhelming in nature, and slice it like a block of cheese or a loaf of bread, or a whole vegetable.

Break it down and watch the overwhelm reduce as you step further up the ladder to get 'all over it', rather than it being 'all over you'. Then you can put these thinly sliced and specific tasks on your Kanban board and work through them – and not all at once!

These techniques are powerful sensemaking tools and they give us the benefit of visibility and perspective.

Now I'm not a big horoscope follower, but when my friend Leigh read this one out to me one day, I thought that Oscar and Jonathan Cainer had nailed it!

'An adventurer who was chasing the Northern Lights said, "You never realise how big the sky is until you try looking at all of it at once." This sums up the message ... [that] life often feels too vast to comprehend; we'll never make sense of our chaotically interconnected world. Perhaps the key to unlocking the bigger picture is to limit our focus into manageable chunks. By arming ourselves with facts, we can build a more comprehensive understanding.'

Takeaways

1. **Notice and name the expectations you have.** Many of our internal commitments are invisible and unknown to us.

2. **Write it down.** Get the information out of your head and stop it spinning and multiplying. Get perspective by seeing it before your eyes.

3. **Reframe the standard you're going for.** Does it really have to be that good, perfect, ideal? Is there an actual need or request for every single thing on your to-do list? Consider how tasks got there in the first place. Were you asked specifically, because …

4. **Check you're not over-volunteering.** As we keep offering to do things, saying 'yes' or 'pick me', know what these additional commitments can add to our physical load as well as the mental load of remembering them and doing them.

5. **Protect some time.** Keep some space in your truck! Instead of filling every square of it, let some space be empty so that it breathes. Give yourself some buffer time between tasks, jobs or projects.

Juggling Work
(Prioritise the work)

OMG, by the way, this chapter took me FOREVER to write because … you know, juggling!

I've started and stopped it about eight times; doing a little bit and then stopping and then dropping it and picking it up a few days later and having another start at it and then dropping it while I was trying to do six other things! I got there … I got it written, but at what cost, what delay, what craziness in the meantime?

I checked the dictionary about the whole thing of juggling.

To juggle means:

- ☆ Throwing and catching several objects simultaneously. (Yes, I was certainly trying to do that.)

- ☆ The act of rearranging things to give a misleading impression. (Yes, ok, in between coaching calls, meetings and dinner with my husband, there was a bit of 'everything's under control' when I was, you know, JUGGLING!)

★ Hold with difficulty and balance insecurely. (OK, yes, you've got me here too. It was tricky holding everything, balancing high-wire style and not feeling like I truly was in control of what I was working on!)

★ Throw, catch and keep in the air several things simultaneously. (Ahh yes, that was me, throwing stuff around!)

… so says the Dictionary app on my phone!

In our effort to get things done, and plenty of them, we can pick up things throughout a day and hold on to them, juggling them the whole day. This workload we carry is often referred to as our 'work in progress'. But we usually have too much work in progress than we can handle.

Sometimes the day might start with good intentions of only doing so much and then an emergency happens or an interruption crops up that threatens the whole schedule of what you were planning to do.

Do we really need to do all of the things we think we do? Who said? What expectations and standards are we holding? What are we trying to do? And why are we trying to do it?

If we can't focus on things, or find ourselves stretched or pulled in all directions, maybe we're juggling too much. And maybe, as the definition says, we're trying to give a misleading impression that everything is just fine and that we can cope.

Perhaps the things we're juggling – like responsibilities, voluntary commitments, agreements, tasks, chores, routines, roles and 'OK, I'll do its' are things we have willingly taken on, not realising the impact they are having on our feelings of overwhelm.

And if we've already got plenty on, are we aware of how our juggling can cause more overwhelm or at least make us feel like we're not making progress?

Research in the *Harvard Business Review* ('What Makes Some People More Productive Than Others') revealed some insightful answers. Nearly 20,000 people from six continents completed a survey and the results suggested two BIG points for us to take note of:

Working longer hours does not necessarily mean higher personal productivity.

What the heck?! You mean working longer, getting up earlier, pushing through lunch breaks, staying back ... those longer hours don't equate to higher personal productivity?

Instead, 'working smarter is the key to accomplishing more of your top priorities each day'.

The highest personal productivity results belonged to people who:

- 'planned their work based on their top priorities

- acted with a definite objective

- developed effective techniques for managing a high volume of information and tasks

- understood the needs of their colleagues (for short meetings, responsive communications, and clear directions)'.

So, it's not just one thing to remedy our workload, overload, overwhelm and juggling. It's a number of things that combined, help us tackle and achieve the things we want and need to achieve.

There will always be things to do. But what we can change is how *much* we are juggling.

The premise that we should stop juggling probably won't 'land' with many people. How could they get done what they need to without at least a bit of juggling?

You know, walking for exercise, walking the dog at the same time, and listening to an audio book. Now that's smart juggling. Just keep a look out for the traffic and other potential safety hazards.

Driving to an event, listening to a mediation? That's not good juggling. Crazy. There's a warning label on those recordings which say, 'Don't listen to this track while driving or operating machinery,' so that's a big 'no' to that kind of juggling.

But there's also the juggling of sequence, having a number of balls up in the air, things that are on the go.

When we need to mail a parcel, drop off some charity donations, pick up the cat from the vet, collect some champagne for the Saturday night catch up with friends, collect some prescriptions for medication and stop by to check in on a relative, it's potentially all possible. Just not all at once!

The sequence then is crucial.

Jugglers don't just throw a bunch of balls up in the air to see which ones they can grab. There is a sequence to juggling and learning juggling.

First you throw and catch one ball in one hand, say the left. And you practice this for about five minutes, going for consistent speed and height, almost to the point of success where you could do it without looking at it. 'Looking through it,' is the advice a former Cirque du Soleil juggler gave me. They'd gone from juggling balls, clubs, and swords in circus tents across the world, to the corporate world helping people juggle their lives and responsibilities better. 'Adopt a kind of distant vision, looking through and ahead, rather than up and down at the ball. Yes, use your peripheral vision,' said the juggler.

Once you've mastered that one ball throw, you're allowed to cross the ball and throw it from the left to the right.

Master that and then you can introduce a second ball. The second ball launches shortly after the first. And this time you throw and catch the second ball with the right hand. So, after you've practiced that for a while, you've got this rhythm or tempo happening:

Throw throw / catch catch.

It's rhythmic and manageable, but yes, as you're learning, balls still fall all over the place.

Then it's the double cross over. Left ball to right hand, right ball to left hand.

Manageable, after some practice.

After you've mastered that, you introduce ... drum roll ... THE THIRD BALL. You hold two in one hand.

This is where the term 'juggling' comes to life. All sorts of crazy is possible here. Now the ball that was in the left goes to the right, the ball in the right goes to the left AND THEN launch the third ball so now it goes:

Throw throw / catch / throw / catch / throw / … and carry on.

In the words of Gloria Estefan, 'The rhythm is going to get you!' The thing about juggling is, when you're learning it, it can absolutely be overwhelming. But it is learnable. Trying to juggle more than three balls needs a year or six at an acrobatics and clown academy. Even more adventurous folks juggle different things like bigger balls, knives, chain saws, bowling balls and fruit. Amusing performers and comedians show us how to cut fruit with the chainsaws and knives – this is next level juggling. Do not try it at home!

Juggling is a skill and we can learn it. How we apply it to our lives though, can see us trying to cope with six or 12 different things at once, instead of just one, two or three.

If you're going to juggle, keep it small, manageable and all within sight – peripheral vision, right, just as the juggler advised.

When I'm juggling tasks, and I'm using Kanban to visualise my work and keep it in sight, I keep the number of 'balls in the air' or tasks in progress to three. Yes, just three. If something else comes along that's urgent, something from my current three has to go back into the backlog, to allow this new one in.

Juggling things becomes a problem when we simply don't know how many balls we have up in the air. How many things are we expected to do, or are we expecting to do? Without knowing, we can take another thing and another thing and another thing on and next thing ... overwhelm. We can't hold all the balls and we end up ...

Dropping one

If we're trying to do a few things at once, or at the same time, or in the same day, it's highly likely we won't be able to keep 'all our balls in the air'. Our plans or expectations were better than reality, or perhaps the conditions changed: the traffic was bad, the pharmacist was slow, the charity shop was closed. Then our plans kind of fall about, we 'drop a few balls'.

This metaphor of 'having balls up in the air' is a common one. Our language expresses it when we say we are 'juggling', just before we hit 'struggling' on the Ladder of Overwhelm shared earlier.

If we can't see them all and don't know what's up in the air, how can we know when we need to start them, do them, finish them or tidy up after them?

This awareness or oversight is crucial if you're going to continue juggling but in a more measured and moderate way.

If juggling isn't going to be deleted from your way of handling overwhelm, at least gather up some of the best practice juggling techniques to make the most of it.

Good jugglers are often asked to carry more. The more we continue to hold and carry things, multiple things, the more we are given or expected to carry.

One or two things, then three, then slot in the fourth and next thing you have six or seven errands to run in what was initially going to be a 15-minute round trip.

When we do things well, appear capable, deliver on time every time, make things happen, and present a constructed reality that seems all of these things, it's no wonder people load on more.

Give the juggler more to juggle. Let's see what they're made of! Until, no, there is nothing more they can carry. They are tired, low on resilience, grieving, sad, exhausted, burnt out, sleep deprived, worrying, overthinking and juggling. All at once. Don't let it get to this.

Prioritising the priorities

Does a 'to do' list ever end up finished? Do we ever get to the end? It's more likely we keep adding to it.

And hands up if you've added something to it AFTER you've done it, just so you can tick it off!!? Come on … I sure have. It's the joy of progressing that we are after.

The problem is our to-do list may be in need of a haircut! Giving your to-do list a haircut, prune or trim is a great task for keeping overwhelm at bay.

Several times a day, I'll revisit my backlog or list of things to do on my Kanban board, to see if they are still needed; really needed.

Some of them drift off into the background; others come into the foreground and they become part of my greater focus. Get the scissors out and decide what's not needed anymore. Perhaps it got done as a by-product of something else; maybe someone else did it; perhaps the opportunity has passed and it's not needed; or ... maybe people won't know that it's not been done.

Grooming or tidying up our list is a responsible thing to do. It keeps us across what we've got on, and helps it stay relevant and current. Otherwise, we could be doing things that are wasteful and unnecessary.

In one of my very first job roles working in local government, I learned a great lesson about prioritising and re-prioritising, this 'grooming' our list of to-dos.

Patsy, the head of the family care services unit next to my office, had folders on her desk that were labelled:

- sooner

- later

- sometime

- never.

I've never forgotten them! But it was her regular reviewing – many times a day – of her folders that impressed me.

She would check what was in her folders and whether the tasks were done, not done, still needed, and whether they were still in the right place.

Her humour about something being done 'sooner' rather than 'later' used to make me laugh. She was always into the 'sooner' folder, her highest priorities.

The 'sometime' and 'never' folders didn't get much action; tasks would drift in there and be left to disappear, simply not needed.

Now, many years later, I still think of my tasks as things that need to be done sooner, later, sometime, never and I give more time and focus to the 'sooner' pile or column. Thanks Patsy!

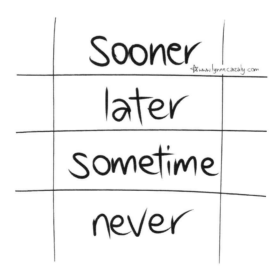

Focusing on one thing vs many things

Multitasking: it's a dangerous work practice and a likely contributor to overwhelm. Even if we think we're pretty good at it, we're sadly and unproductively mistaken! I know you might be thinking, 'but my day is constant multitasking, Lynne,' or 'isn't that just how we work these days, multiple tasks at once?!' Believe it or not, multitasking is an evil. It steals and splits our attention and precious energy across multiple tasks.

It FEELS like we're attending to multiple tasks, but our attention diminishes and it's not equally split 50/50 across two tasks. The drain of multitasking is worse; it's more like 10/10, or 20/20, with 80% of our attention and effort wasted in recovering each time we switch.

Trying to juggle too much and switching between the things we have to do, isn't good for us or our productivity.

- ☆ Multitasking leads to as much as a 40% drop in productivity.[2]

- ☆ Multitaskers lost significant amounts of time as they switched between multiple activities and lost even more time as the tasks became increasingly complex.[3]

And it's not good for our smarts!

- ☆ Multitasking causes a 10% drop in IQ.[4]

- ☆ Multitasking affects your brain much like smoking marijuana or going without sleep for a night. Participants who multitasked during cognitive tasks dropped as many as 15 IQ points and fell to the average range of an 8-year-old child according to research from the Institute of Psychiatry in London.[5]

Work takes us longer.

- Multitaskers not only take 50% longer to accomplish a single task but they also make up to 50% more errors, says, John Medina in his brilliant book *Brain Rules*.

- In one study, a group of Microsoft workers took, on average, 15 minutes to return to serious mental tasks, like writing reports or computer code, after responding to incoming e-mail or instant messages. They'd strayed off to reply to other messages or browse news, sports or entertainment web sites.[6]

And it's a contributor to stress.

- Multitasking has been tied to higher stress levels. Gloria Mark and Stephen Voida of the University of California measured the heart rates of employees with and without continuous access to work-related email. They found that employees who were constantly connected to email stayed in a perpetual 'high alert' mode and experienced higher heart rates. Those without the constant stream of emails did less multitasking and were less stressed as a result.[7]

We never really get up to speed on something before we try to catch something else we're juggling and we lose the momentum.

What do we do when the desire to do more than one thing is so strong? Of the 'everything' we have to work on, and the 'many things' we might like to multitask on, it's the act of a DECISION that gives us the greatest opportunity to get up and all over our overwhelm.

Staying down in among the juggle and struggle of many things at once doesn't suit how our brains were designed.

Our mono-tasking minds LOVE doing just one thing and focusing intently on it. It's our distracted and anxious minds that wrongly think we can take on multiple things at once.

If we think that all of our tasks are important, then the 2 × 2 matrix by Dwight Eisenhower and Dr Steven Covey might help you classify whether something needs to be done, now … or if it can wait until later.

MORE IMPORTANT	Schedule a specific time	No time like the present
LESS IMPORTANT	Eliminate, postpone or quick win	Delegate or divide and conquer
Eisenhower / Covey Matrix	LESS URGENT	MORE URGENT

This tool, originally shared by Dwight Eisenhower and then popularised in Dr Stephen Covey's book *The Seven Habits of Highly Effective People*, has helped so many people prioritise what they're working on.

We can consider whether something is less important or more important and less urgent or more urgent. And each of the four squares where we might place ourselves and the task at hand has some suggestions for how to prioritise. This tool can help us classify or sort, but it is still up to us to DECIDE. Decide means to 'kill off alternatives', to make up one's mind.

If we're working on more than one thing, then we haven't really decided. Sometimes it's less about the many tasks, and more about the fact we need to decide. Then once a decision is made and you are on the other side of it, things get easier; they really do.

What's one thing you could decide and focus on right now?

Making such a decision can help relieve the feelings of struggling or juggling, and get yourself up to progressing on the Ladder of Overwhelm.

How many loops have you got open?

There's a great meme that circles the internet about how many tabs we have open in our web browser. Some people are focused with just one or two and other people remark about how they have 18 or 35.

And this is a fine example of what it's like walking about with an overload of work or an overload of mental activity. You have multiple screens open in your mind – like having 17 different tabs open on your desktop browser.

Some of them never even get closed because the task or activity is still outstanding. But the same thing happens in our mind, and we try to work and get through the day with so many things open.

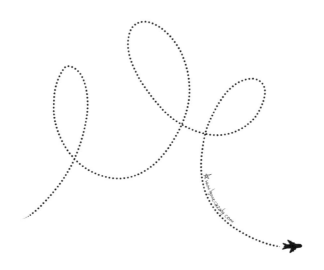

Psychology often refers to this as having an 'open loop'. The point or project is open, in progress, and instead of working on it and closing it, closing the loop, we continue working on it, carrying it around in our load. And then open up another project, another loop. Before long we have plenty of loops open and not many loops closed.

This is reinforced in the business world where productivity and efficiency are the focus by saying 'stop starting, start finishing'. In other words, close some loops before you open others.

Beware of 'bike shedding'

Not everything you want to work on can or will be of equal importance. There's a kind of 'triage' we can apply to our work, just as patients presenting at a hospital emergency department are classified by the nursing and medical team depending on the severity of their injuries.

Even if we persist and insist that, 'yes, EVERYTHING is important', we may well be engaging in the practice of 'bike shedding'.

Bike shedding is a term based on Parkinson's Law – The Law of Triviality.

It suggests that we can give unequal or unreasonable weight to less important things. It would be like a committee working on the building and construction of a hospital and spending so much time on the materials being used for the staff bike-shed. It might have some importance, but not at the loss of attention going towards the health, medical, patient and administrative aspects of the business.

Software developers I've worked with over the years have frequently dropped the phrase into conversations and meetings, 'Be sure we're not bike-shedding here,' or 'Um, people, are we bike-shedding perchance?' or my favourite, 'BS people! Bike-shed!' This is a quick reminder to refocus on the stuff that's truly valuable and important for us to work on ... now.

Takeaways

1. Reduce your work in progress (WIP)
If we're trying to manage eight things at once but only have time for four, something will give. So, it's time to prioritise. The practice of 'stop starting, start finishing' is strong here, because we'll be more effective and productive and less overwhelmed if we reduce the number of things we're trying to do.

2. Identify the value of your key tasks
Understand why you're doing what you're doing. Be clear about the value, outcomes and results prioritising this work will bring.

3. Readjust your expectations
Everything may not flow smoothly, work faultlessly or happen in a way that's timely. When we work or collaborate with others, we may need to be more flexible.

4. Pause the performance
Take a break, a day, a weekend, or an hour, to reset. Close the curtain, take a break, or call intermission or interval. Even the best jugglers need downtime. The world's theatres have a period of time known as a 'dark day' or 'the theatre is dark'. This is when there is no performance scheduled.

5. Get a new set of balls
Maybe it's time to look at what you're juggling and whether you want to be juggling this stuff anyway. It's a big question about some of the biggest priorities in your life.

Switching Work
(Focus on the task)

Esther was at the annual industry conference and had been looking forward to the break from work (and home) for weeks. As she sat at a round table with white linen tablecloths, played with her lanyard, and flicked through the conference program app on her phone, she thought she'd better check her email while she was waiting. Who knew what was happening back at the office!

She refreshed the mail app; nothing much there, so she switched over to see what her friends were up to on Facebook. Then a jump over to Instagram for a quick scroll through the images from the weekend. Then the conference started. It was that sponsor talk at the start, so she got her laptop out and started reading through a couple of job applications for the role she was recruiting for.

The first speaker of the conference started, so she listened to them but kept her hands on the keyboard of her laptop. She noticed her parents had sent a text message, so she opened that and read it and replied. And then a notification *appeared on her laptop that a file she'd been working on had been changed by a colleague, so she opened up the file to check what the changes were.*

The first speaker wasn't that interesting by this time, so she continued reading the CVs from the job applicants, sent a 'who else is here at the conference' tweet on Twitter so she looked like she was actually working, and searched through the conference app for what time morning tea was. She remembered there was a factory outlet store near the convention centre so she thought she might slip in there in the next break and see if they had a pair of trainers to go with her new gym gear.

The audience applauded so she joined in but didn't really know what she was clapping for. She hadn't really heard that much of the speaker.

Then it was morning tea and Esther felt like she'd been so busy already and the day had barely started. How would she stay focused and interested in everything until the gala dinner at the conference that night?

Let's have a reality check about overwhelm.

Our understanding and definition of reality has likely changed in recent years with the rise and rise of the reality genre. Or as the producers and creators of some of the reality shows say, 'structured reality', or better still, 'constructed reality'. This is where, say, three contestants on one of the bachelor dating shows have to sit down together by the pool and are briefed to chat on a particular topic, like if Donald will get a rose from Veronica. And if the producers don't think it's quite there ... not quite entertaining enough, it's 'CUT! DO IT AGAIN'! It's not really real; it's made up and then made to look real.

What we believe to be real — even in our own reality — let's face it, is quite produced and constructed.

And how we live our daily lives is quite produced and constructed too. We choose daily outfits to wear, we apply makeup, style our hair, pack a particular lunch, drive a particular route in a specific brand of car, listening to a particular podcast or genre of music, have coffee from a favoured cafe in a specific style of our choosing ... and on goes the daily production of our daily life.

Is it any wonder then that the threat of having to do a reality check could scare us or make us rush for a lengthy stay at Denial Resort or a cosy retreat at Delusion Cottages for the weekend?

Getting real with our overwhelm could take some cutting through, you know, like weeds, jungle, undergrowth and overgrowth. It's machete time, where we slash and cut through all of that stuff that's hiding the actual true real reality.

The cost of distraction

Checking your phone during a meeting is a productivity, focus and attention killer.

We think we can be present in the meeting AND scroll, check and read ... but no.

- ☆ Heavy media multitaskers easily get distracted and are not able to filter out what's not relevant to their current goal where there are multiple sources of information from the external world or emerging out of memory.[8]

- ☆ According to a 2009 study from Western Washington University, people who are busy doing two things at once don't even see noticeable things right in front of them. The researchers call this 'inattentional blindness'.[9]

Our IQ drops and we develop 'inattentional blindness'.

We lose the ability to judge what information is valuable or important. It's probably why we think some speakers deliver boring segments, meetings have boring parts or workshops have boring sections. But shock, horror ... it may not be boring at all!

It's possible our ability to make sense has been interrupted. What others deem important ... we don't. Then it switches over; they check their phone and get distracted, and we're paying attention. We notice the important things; they don't.

Focus, attention, IQ and cognition will be better, stronger and the work will be achieved quicker when we focus.

The danger of 'as long as it takes'

Tasks that have no time limit take as long as they take. Which could be forever! Parkinson's Law – and this is different to the other Parkinson's Law mentioned earlier about trivial work – says work expands to fit the time available. If we say we will set aside two hours to <insert one of your tasks> then that's how long it's going to take!

Our perception of time can be distorted. We can find it difficult to know how much time has passed: was it 30 minutes or 3 hours? Was it 5 minutes or 45?

We know time distorts for us because sometimes time feels like it's passing slowly, perhaps when we're bored or under stimulated. And at other times, time feels like it's passing so quickly, that feeling of 'running out of time' … usually when we are overstimulated.

To help us with time, why don't we get someone or rather, some-thing to keep track of it?

Here is one of the most popular and most successful techniques for helping us focus: setting a time limit.

'Timeboxing' as it is often called.

It's been one of the best tools that has helped me work each day, that's for sure, and it most certainly helps me control my overwhelm and helps me move to the top of the overwhelm ladder to progress and achieve!

Timeboxing has helped me write seven books, plan and prepare for workshops, research, write blog posts, and generally get things done.

It's a key way of reimagining our work because if we haven't used timeboxing before, it's a new thing! We may only imagine what it's like. If we've been more of a slogging hard worker, pushing on and working another hour or two on a task, it most certainly is different.

This is how I work and I love it.

If you haven't tried a time limit or timebox, try it today.

I use the timer on my phone or simply say, 'Hey Siri, set a timer for 25 minutes,' and then I start working.

Why 25 minutes?

25 minutes is an almost magic time duration. It's based on the success of the Pomodoro Technique, and it's enough to get you going on something but not so much that it drains you or takes you down rabbit holes. This time management technique – by

Francesco Cirillo – originated in the 1980s. Using a timer – of usually 25 minutes in length – you work uninterrupted for that interval, and then when the timer goes off, you stop and take a short break. 'Pomodoro' comes from the Italian word 'tomato' because Cirillo used one of those cute little kitchen timers that was shaped like a tomato and only went for 25 minutes!

So, after the 25 minutes, stop and either do something else or have a short break. I have a wander around, get a drink, check my email or go outside and breathe some fresh air.

Then it's back for another 25 minutes.

Longer timeboxes work too, say, up to 90 minutes which can work well with our normal rhythms of attention and energy.

If you already know about this technique for working ... do you use it? Really use it?

It works because ... you know, distraction! In the article 'The Two Things Killing Your Ability to Focus' in *Harvard Business Review*, author William Treseder claims that being overwhelmed with distractions is eroding our ability to process, recharge and refocus. We are in a 'hyperconnected' state and often unable to maintain focus long enough to carry out effective work. (Oh, and the second thing that kills our ability to focus is dysfunctional meetings!)

Try it out. Set a timer, start working and don't stop until the timer goes off.

Boxing time can also be done in advance. Many people find that blocking out time in their diaries and schedules helps them plan ahead and commit to thinking, working, preparing, chasing up and following through.

The pressure to take on more

'Could you just …?'
'Would you be able to …?'
'Who's going to help me …?'

We can often be faced with requests and questions to take on or do more. And a request for help, support or a contribution can be a common way we are distracted and lose our focus.

'Can you look at this for me?'
'When can you fix …?'
'Have you got a minute?'

But we don't need to jump in and take on additional tasks nor apologise repeatedly for not taking them on.

Don't take them on.

Don't be sorry about it.

The 'volunteer technique' comes to mind. A crusty old leader at a charity I worked at would seek volunteers at meetings for additional, unpaid work. He knew a number of people at the table would 'volunteer'. Actually, it's not volunteering; it's pressuring, guilting and shaming, expecting someone to 'fill the space' or step in to the need that's been created. Anyone who wants to help relieve another's pain, reduce stress, nurture another or care for another would step in at this charity. How could you not? And it is often the same people.

And it adds to our overload and overwhelm. And it was unpaid. And extra hours of work.

But volunteering via pressure, guilt and shame isn't going to remedy or reduce overwhelm. It only adds to it.

With a reality check, we can see what we're doing by breaking the boundary we tried to set up and we allowed the water to come trickling, then flooding in. And then it's overwhelm time.

Sometimes we try with the end of one year and the start of another. We berate ourselves that 'this year' we will define our boundaries better; be stronger; say no; to prioritise and practice self-care better.

But these things are all harder to do when overwhelm is … overwhelming.

Tune in to music for focus

Music is wonderful for recreation, entertainment and general listening. But did you know it's also a powerful productivity tool?

It's brilliant for helping us focus AND it's a stress management and mood regulation tool too!

When you're overwhelmed – with work, life, emotions or situations – what is your 'go to' tune that you know calms you down?

We know about 'Eye of the Tiger' and 'We Are the Champions' as rousing songs that motivate teams, but what about the reverse ... the more calming and focusing effects of music?

My go-to track is Bullitnuts, 'Heavy Air'. It might not mean much to you, but it just works for me – familiar, calming, groovy little beat, no lyrics, a bass rhythm. When I read some of the research about beats and rhythm and their effect on us, it made sense as to why I liked this track so much.

Researchers at Stanford University School of Medicine found that 'music engages the areas of the brain involved with paying attention, making predictions and updating the event in memory. Peak brain activity occurred during a short period of silence between musical movements – when seemingly nothing was happening.'

So listening to music is good for paying attention; and the silences between tunes or movements are even better for helping bring things together for us and make sense!

I've used my favourite track of music when driving and reading and when I have a break from work. It works for me because it's familiar.

Deep Patel, in the article 'These 6 Types of Music Are Known to Dramatically Improve Productivity', lists 'classical, nature, cinematic, video game, music between 50–80 beats per minute, and your favourite music' as some of the best for us.

Emily Conklin agrees in '12 Ways That Music Makes You More Productive at Work', saying that music does things like lifts our mood, makes repetitive tasks more enjoyable, gets you into a flow state, speeds up your work, reduces distractions, drowns out your colleagues, stops us clock watching … and adds a virtual 'do not disturb' sign. So. Much. Good.

But it's not all about productivity!

If there is one track of music to help relieve stress and have the best effect on us overwhelmed types, it's 'Weightless' by Marconi Union.

Oh, my goodness, it turns out that this piece of music relieves stress and anxiety by up to 65%!

How does a piece of music do that? It seems that music's thera-peutic nature holds the key. Mindlab, the research firm associated with the study says:

'Certain pieces of music do indeed possess the power to calm even the most stressed-out individuals by soothing frazzled minds and relaxing bodies. The study confirmed certain music has the capacity to lower heart rate, slow breathing and decrease levels of the stress hormone "cortisol" in the blood.'

The 'Weightless' track by Marconi Union

- induced greater relaxation levels in participants than a massage (up by 6%)

- induced an 11% increase in relaxation over all other relaxing music tracks

- was subjectively rated as more relaxing than any other music by all the participants and

- has a greater ability to induce relaxation than having a cup of tea, going for a walk and playing video games.

Music works deeply in our brain, stimulating regions associated with emotions. It's perhaps more effective than we realise at combating stress, helping us memorise information, learn a language and for an overwhelming situation of distraction ... focusing our attention!

BUT DON'T LISTEN to this track while driving because it also made people quite drowsy. That could be dangerous. There's a 10-hour extended version of the track on YouTube if you do need it for helping with sleep!

Once I heard about this music, I downloaded it straight away so it lives in my personal music list. I've used it many times knowing that it will have a positive effect on my heart rate and blood pressure and my general feeling of wellbeing, especially when I'm feeling stressed, overloaded, overwhelmed or in a state of 'Argh!'

In your own cafe

Do you find cafés productive places to work? Perhaps it's that we are away from our regular home, desk or office space where other responsibilities and distractions can interrupt our attempts to focus our attention.

Many people laude the vibey sounds and the music – sometimes barely recognisable – in their favourite or indeed any café. For many it's this white noise that gives them time and space to focus. If you can't get out of your home or office or usual location to get to a café – hi there to Kim and Sal who live 450kms away from their nearest town on a remote farm station in outback Australia – here's something that's got focus and productivity all over it.

I've used Coffitivity (at www.coffitivity.com) for years – for when I'm working alone or when I need a creative environment in the workshops I'm leading.

Choose a Coffitivity soundtrack and you'll recreate the ambient sounds of cafes — and you can choose whether you want a morning rush kind of sound or an afternoon bistro sound from Brazil!

Just press play and the magic starts! Creating a coffee shop sound is highly creative and productive for us, and can be strangely calming and comforting, particularly if we are missing our usual coffee shop or cafe hangouts and visits. We can use it as a pre-emptive strategy to keep overload and overwhelm at bay.

These sound effects can be played over your computer speakers or plug in your head-phones and create your own world!

It turns out that a little bit of distraction, like the ambient sound in a cafe is highly productive, creative and effective. In 'Is Noise Always Bad? Exploring the Effects of Ambient Noise on Creative Cognition', researchers Mehta, Zhu and Cheema found that a 'moderate level of ambient noise is conducive to creative cognition.'

So turn on some café and music sounds and reap the benefits of both distraction management plus a creativity boost!

Takeaways

1. **Notice distractions.** Who or what seems to be your go-to distraction ... and how long does it take you to get back to the original task?

2. **Try out timeboxing;** it's the best productivity and focusing tool of all of them. Try a couple of timeboxes a day and see how focusing becomes easier to master.

3. **More music.** Rediscover music if you've lost touch with what you like. And get started on some ambient sounds as the best resolve for distractions and overwhelm.

4. **What's the do-over?** If you could start afresh, where would you put new boundaries in? What would they be? Think of each area of your life and consider time, responsibilities, behaviours, actions and expectations.

5. **Where is reality hiding from you?** What's in the way of the really big reality for you? Is there something that you don't want to see, don't like to admit or would rather not own? That's ok. Just know that there might be great learning and growth – and freedom – on the other side of the reality check about the reality check.

Sensemaking the Work

Switch on your sensemaking and ask:

What does the work mean for you?

OK, someone may have delegated something to us, and we have to do it.

Or, we've made a commitment to someone and we are delivering on that.

Perhaps we're doing study for a particular purpose and reason. What is that? Why is it important to us?

And then anything else on our 'to do' list: why do you think it's there?

This is not to make us start deleting things from our goals and task lists, but to understand – and reimagine – why we're working on something, or choosing to say 'yes' to it … and taking it on.

In some of the work I do with businesses and teams, we often spend time in workshops determining why something is on our 'to do' list, what the outcomes are from it. In strategy sessions we do this too, and use it as a sensemaking activity. It helps stop endless tasks being added to the list! Here's the three-column tool I use:

TASK What am I doing?	MEANING Why does it matter?	OUTCOME What will happen as a result of doing it?
Cleaning out my office	To get organised where I do important work	I'll feel calmer, able to find everything
Collecting information for my tax	I don't like numbers but it's a legal requirement	Refund? I'll be up to date and have met legal obligation

It asks us to think about:

1. The task: what am I doing?

2. The meaning: why does it matter?

3. The outcome: what will happen as a result of doing it?

We don't need to write everything down, just a few and soon we can pick up the pattern that tasks either have meaning and outcomes for us, or they are 'busy work' or could perhaps be delayed or delegated.

What is really is going on?

Who really is adding things to my to-do list?

How many hours a week do I spend helping with the kid's home-work and costumes?

When did I last have my health checks?

What will it take for me to do a check on my finances?

How is my brother coping with his new job?

When did I last see my dear friend?

...

These important things often get pushed to the bottom of our overwhelmed and overloaded list as we deal with the latest or next challenge, drama and trauma in our life. But rather than ignoring them, we need to prioritise them.

Making sense of our overwhelm – the reality of our overload – is going to be enlightening, perhaps a little frightening – but only through this clarity can sense be made, actions taken and a powerful trust return to the design and living of our own lives.

 1. Visualise

Get it out of your head, externalise information rather than internalising it.

Kanban board 'To Do' or 'Backlog' list.

2. Prioritise

There's too much in flight, too much going on, too much juggling. Prioritise your Top 3 for today. I use a 3 + 1 method, where I write my three priorities for the project, day or morning, and then a fourth one that's a rest or reward or joy for me. It's there for me to do once I'm done with the other three.

Template/Tool for 3 + 1

3+1
☆ www.lynnecazaly.com

1.

_____

2.

_____

3.

_____

+1

3. *Focus*

What's the best use of your time now? Rather than juggling and switching, set a timer and get started on a task. When you do get distracted by thoughts or ideas or other incoming distractions – and you will – SIDETASK by writing them down on a notepad next to you. Don't start the task. Focus on the 'Doing' column.

Understanding how we work, can provide us with some great clues into our overload and overwhelm ... particularly if overwhelm shows up at work, during work or doing work. With visualising, prioritising and focusing, we're able to redesign the work and outsmart our overwhelm.

the OVERWHELM	❶ Pause	❷ Locate	❸ Relabel
	Re-define the overwhelm		
the WORK	❹ Vizualise	❺ Prioritise	❻ Focus
	Re-design the work		
			⭐www.lynnecazzaly.com

Download these templates and other resources at
www.lynnecazaly.com.au/argh

3

Aaah!

www.lynnecazaly.com

Part 3
The Load of Information

Introduction

When it hits you, that information overload feeling, what do you do? Panic? Push on through? Look at your phone?

None of these are helpful.

The feeling of overload, that 'full sponge' feeling isn't pleasant.

Disengagement, distraction and withdrawal are all behaviours connected with information overload. We don't need to suffer.

We've looked at two perspectives of emotional overwhelm and workload ... now let's cleverly outsmart overwhelm from this third perspective – information overload.

Just think, if we can:

✰   take in more information,

✰   process it more readily,

✰   store it smartly,

✰   retrieve it swiftly, and

✰   apply in it more efficient and productive ways,

... then information overload won't be a problem or pain point for us anymore.

We'll conquer it. And we can.

Endless Information
(Filter information)

How do you start your day? Are you overloaded before you even begin?

A group of friends I chatted to said they listen to podcasts, audio books, interviews and radio programs on their daily commutes to work or the school drop off, while they're exercising, walking, relaxing, cooking, and cleaning.

There's nothing wrong with this. It can be entertaining, educational and a great use of time.

What we need to be aware of is how we fill up our sponge or truck with content and information that we potentially need to absorb, synthesise and digest. Then we arrive at work or start work on our project and we're faced with even more content and information to absorb, synthesise and digest!

Argh!

No wonder overload comes a-knocking!

It's possible we could be overloaded before the day begins, or soon after we get started.

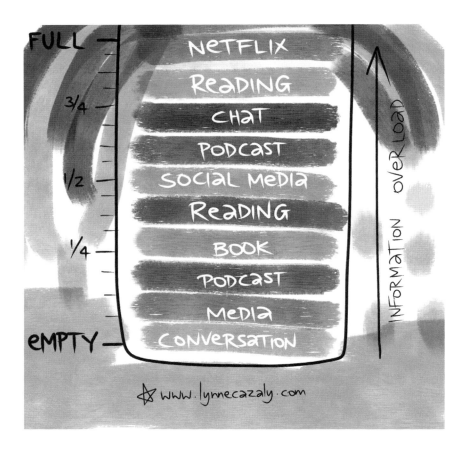

We have to do something. Until an artificial intelligence or scientific leading light finds us a device that helps us manage the load with a brain implant, the tap of a button or swipe of an app, we'll have to do something about it ourselves. We need to make sure we're equipped with the skills that will make us better humans for the future. We don't have to do a lot, but we do need to do something – different.

And employers need to do something too.

Leaders can't keep giving their people more and more information and yet not give them the guidance, training or skill development to know *how* to handle it.

It's an employer's responsibility to further equip the people who work for them with the skills and techniques they need to do their job even better in this crazy information-rich world.

Rather than sending people off on generic leadership programs that rarely shift the dial on engagement or culture, there's an opportunity with cognitive load coping to equip a team with skills that will truly help them work smarter not harder when it comes to working with all that information.

The load on the mind

The Institute for the Future identified 'cognitive load coping' as one of the top skills we'll need for 2020 and beyond. 'Cognitive' or cognition is how we understand things, store, process and retrieve information and make decisions. When that capability is overloaded, we struggle to take more information in or process more information. So to be able to manage or 'cope' with cognitive load is a good thing, powerful, impactful, and helpful for us to live our daily lives, learning, adapting and coping.

The theory about cognitive load was developed in the late 1980s by fellow Australian and educational psychologist John Sweller. His research centred on problem solving and the idea that the heavy load on our brain for working memory – particularly when learning something – can be reduced via good information and instructional design.

His work built on an original and often-quoted paper from the 1950s by American psychologist, George Armitage Miller. Miller, among other things, coined the term 'chunk' for working with smaller pieces of information in an effort to remember them ... like how telephone numbers are grouped in a kind of rhythm when we remember them. For example, it's easier to recall 37 24 06 rather than 372406. That's three smaller chunks versus one big one.

But who hasn't felt the symptoms of information overload, that feeling as if you're 'drowning in it', your brain is like a soaking wet sponge that can't take any more in?

In the article 'The Ways Your Brain Manages Overload, and How to Improve Them', author Srini Pillay writes, 'the human brain [is] metaphorically endowed with a vacuum cleaner that sucks up information; a container for short term memory; a blender for integrating information; a memory bank for storing long-term information; a garbage disposal for getting rid of information; and a recycling machine extraordinaire.' That's one heck of a food, err, information processor!

And he continues, 'few people build the habits and lifestyles that allow for their brains to function at their best.'

The pressure of information overload – we experience it daily in meetings, workshops, conversations, arguments, debates, pres-entations and most spectacularly at conferences and learning situations where we *want* to take information on board and act on it, but we find that at varying points – it's all too much. Argh!

Whether cognitive overload hits you gradually or rapidly, the situation is the same: you can't absorb anything more. You're over-loaded. Both your short-term memory and your ability to convert information and store it in your long-term memory for future use and reference are full, swamped and struggling to keep up.

And it's not just when we're reading something or listening to someone. In the modern workplace – and the increasingly remote and online workplace – we get overloaded with information in meetings, often trying to listen to one person (possibly drone on and on). At other times we struggle with the way information is rambling, unstructured, or just too lengthy.

We think we can keep processing, analysing, digesting and synthe-sising all of this information … endlessly, all day, every day.

But it's too often too much. We begin to 'zone out', disengage, get confused and end up after a day of it, feeling exhausted, foggy, 'thick' and zombie-like.

Discriminate, discern and filter

Coping with this information overload is all about 'our ability to discriminate and filter information for importance, and to under-stand how to maximise cognitive functioning using a variety of tools and techniques' (Institute for the Future, Future Work Skills, 2020).

We see people in conferences trying to capture information, either writing frantically or using their phone to snap images of slides that seem to have importance.

That sense of *'I might need this later, I'd better capture it'*, or *'that looks interesting; I'll get a photo and look at it later.'*

In online meetings on Zoom, people grab screenshots of slides full of information for the same intention: I'll look at it later.

But how often do we actually 'look at it later'? When we return to the workplace, get back onto our tasks or return after lunch, we're overloaded with emails, tasks on our to-do lists, packs of information and thoughts on our mind and now we need to process and download all of the information we missed while we were at the meeting/conference/workshop/love-in!

We never seem to catch a break, get ahead of the information or get on the front foot.

And what do we do with it when we look at the information later anyway? Now that we're away from the vital context of the information, its importance diminishes and what we've captured doesn't seem to make as much sense, have as much impact or inspire us as it did back then, in that euphoric moment.

Too often we spend precious evenings or weekends (or worse, holidays!) playing catch up with information that needs to be read, reviewed and revisited so that actions and insights can be gained.

So now we're feeling cognitive overload as well as a dose of guilt and shame: *'Why can't I handle this stuff?'* or *'I need to keep up with it or I'll never get ahead,'* or *'My friends and family never see me because I'm always catching up on reading information.'* No wonder we get overwhelmed.

The idea that information needs to be discriminated and filtered for importance in cognitive load coping can often be overlooked in our daily lives. We might be fearful of the consequences of not having the answers or knowing something or we're desperately trying to cover our butt by making 'everything important' or 'capturing it all' … just in case. But this misstep means we're dealing with too much information all the time. Capturing it all isn't a solution.

Deanne was so pumped and excited about returning to study. She'd completed the enrolment details, paid the first instalment of the course fee, set up a new folder on her computer and been to the local stationery store to buy some new binders, a new leather-look journal and some cool coloured markers. Who doesn't love some new stationery? And given this was a course that would help her with her career, the stationery was a tax deduction, right? Everything was set for the Monday morning kick-off at 9am.

And then it started … the deluge, the flood of information, information, and more information. There were the admin things to do like upload a profile photo, add in a profile description and download the course outlines. There was some shopping to do, ordering a couple of new textbooks. There was a 'get to know you' event at 10.15am to meet other students plus a 'what to expect' session at midday over lunch to learn more about how the program ran. The library was offering a 'how to get the most out of us' session from 2-3pm and she had a 60-minute lecture/workshop to go to where she found out she had a presentation to review, a chapter of the book to read plus six questions to answer. Deanne was not only trying to 'stay on top of' all of the emails and communications from the university, she was also drowning in messages from all of the students on the Slack app channel dedicated to the course. There were hundreds of welcome messages and introductions because the program leaders had suggested people get into the community and introduce themselves. There was so much to read; too much to read. And this was only day one! How was she ever going to juggle studying part time and working part time?

For Deanne, it wasn't just the amount of work, it was also the thinking, remembering, recalling and absorbing all of what she'd just heard. It was difficult to just remember where to go to find certain things, which app did what and where to find out key information for the subjects she'd chosen. The headings for finding information in the university's portal were all looking the same and nothing seemed to make sense.

By mid-afternoon on day one, Deanne realised this wasn't going to be an easy path. It was going to be a struggle! Was she foolish for thinking she could handle work AND study? She was wondering how on earth everybody else manages their time – and their mind – with all of this information. And deeper down, Deanne wondered was she really cut out for this. Perhaps she should get a refund, back out of it all and go back to life as it was.

With these kinds of experiences on day one, week one or even year one of studying, it's no wonder that attrition or drop-out rates from courses range between 7% and 42% depending on the course and the year of study.[10]

When there's too much to handle, the easiest response might be to say, 'I can't handle it. I'm out of here. This isn't for me. I'm done.'

The 'I'm done' statement sounds like we are cooked, roasted, 'done' and baked. And in a way, we are. Our brain feels fried, full of too much information and there isn't any more space to stuff in more content, information or learning.

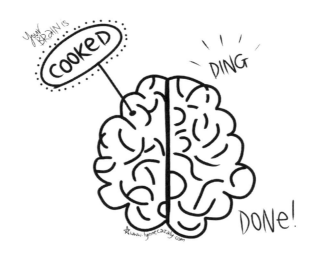

This experience of day one for Deanne is replicated the world over as we all experience this overloaded, fried feeling. It happens when we're starting a new job, moving to a new city, launching a business, studying at school or university, attending a day full of meetings for work, juggling a diary full of tasks, getting through a calendar packed with client appointments, attending a conference of speakers and workshops, logging in for back-to-back online Zoom meetings or tackling and coping with a life full of commitments and things to do! There is that familiar feeling of 'I can't take it anymore!'

Our brain is full and whatever attempts to go into our brain next … doesn't! It overflows and doesn't stick or stay there.

This is cognitive overload. Like the overflowing of a dam wall, rising river waters in times of flood, a monster tide on the full moon or a glass overflowing at the kitchen sink: all of these situations show us what is happening in our brains with information. There's simply too much information for the space that's available.

The way we can handle and respond to cognitive overload is cognitive load coping.

We get cognitively overloaded in two main ways:

1. **Rapidly:** when, say, an expert is delivering a presentation rapid-fire, with lots of data, charts and graphs. Boom! Slam! Bam! Overloaded. Too much to take in. We shutdown.

2. **Gradually:** when we experience the cumulative effects of content adding up and building up throughout the day, meeting after meeting, book after book, online meeting, presentation deck, the kids' homework, the administration bills, the readings for study and education, the blogs for interest, the recipe for dinner. Argh! All of this information ... finally, at the end of the day, when we've tried to keep taking it all in ... it becomes too much. We're zonked, zapped and brain fried. We shutdown.

While we juggle and struggle to cope with the never-ending supply of information, we are doing our best. We're not broken! It's that our brain wasn't designed or didn't evolve to cope with huge amounts of information as we're expecting it to. The brain was best tasked with finding food, chasing or running from threats and eating a much less information-rich diet. Yes, our cave dwelling days may be done but our cave dwelling brain lives on, generation after generation.

So while we might be doing the best we can with what we have, we're also not helping the situation much by doing things like multi-screening (watching TV and using our phones or laptops), multitasking (bathing the kids and checking our emails) or mega-dosing on multiple sources of information at once (listening to a podcast, and researching a presentation, plus checking the football scores).

What else do we do that can make this overload situation feel worse? We switch. From this, to that. In a determined effort to juggle the information and cope with the overload, we may give ourselves a break from one source of information, like reading a school news-letter and quickly switching over to checking through our incoming emails, and then switch over to a tutorial or learning session where we need to take notes to understand what's going on.

This 'switching' – changing from one big activity to another, often unrelated, big activity – confuses and drains our brain. Here we are multitasking again! In an effort to deal with the overload, we don't really make things better. Could we be making things worse … and not even know it?

Imagine that. We start off feeling fairly smart and then after a little while of juggling or switching, we become dumb and dumber! And down our IQ goes, to the equivalent of an 8-year-old – the research from The Institute of Psychiatry in London as we heard about earlier in Juggling Work! What have we missed? While our IQ is dropping, we become less able to determine what's useful information and what's not

There's Deanne, whether on her day one, or day 45, as she juggles multiple lectures, online meetings, team collaborations, online chat channels for each subject, chapter readings, library research … and oh, don't forget to stop by the library, check your emails, collect your assignments and schedule an appointment with your tutor.

As this kind of overloaded day goes on, with our IQ dropping as we multitask, we lose our ability to judge and discern what is valuable or important. We lose interest. What 8-year-old *would* be interested in some of the things we're working on? As we lose IQ, lose the ability to discern, and experience a reduction in our engagement and interest, it makes for a tough situation indeed. Argh!

No wonder we struggle to pay attention in what we THINK are boring meetings, dull reports, droning lectures, endless conference presentations and talk-fests! It turns out they may not be that boring; our 8-year-old IQ just isn't that interested, even if our responsible adult self should be. The information becomes all too much. Argh!

If we reject or ignore – or completely miss – a call to 'pay attention' when it counts, it could be a costly mistake. In effect we have less attention to give when we're overloaded, less effort available to expend, and probably less f*cks to give, thank you Mark Manson, author of *The Subtle Art of Not Giving a F*ck*.

If we persist, push on and keep on driving forward like all good heroes do, it doesn't help us either. Our relentless working continues to overload us. It's like trying to load a truck that's already full; remember Seth Godin's metaphor? There's no more space, no matter how much the driver might like to take more soil to the landscape gardening job.

What to do?

If we realise that our brains aren't coping with the cognitive overload we're putting them under, then we might go a little easier on them and decide to take up some different tasks that will help. We can't keep expecting ourselves to read something once and be able to magically memorise it, synthesise it, analyse it and apply it … we're not all memory champions or quiz show wizards with a genius for retaining ridiculous levels of information.

If you deliberately adopt new and better ways of thinking and working with information – and again let the techniques of sensemaking do some of the work for you – cognitive load will be something you cope with, and get on top of, not get overloaded and ultimately overwhelmed by.

Information isn't slowing down; we'll have to do something about it. And it is on us to manage our own cognitive load. No one is coming to say, 'Here, Deanne, let me handle some of that information for you so you can just sit in the lecture and soak it up.' Deanne, and all of us, can take some deliberate actions and steps to recognise if cognitive load is approaching (remember it may strike us gradually or rapidly) and take pre-emptive steps to remedy and reduce it so we can get on with our daily doings.

Until science fiction becomes fact and we're given removeable microchips to magically store and retrieve information, we can use the techniques ahead to make sense of information overload and sort it out. Then we'll not only cope with it, but we will conquer it!

Five techniques

Here are five techniques to put to work so you'll outsmart over-whelm and in particular, information overload:

1. **Get context, quick: what is this really about?** Identify what this information you're working with is about and why it's important to you, them, it, the situation. When we're working with information, getting the context or big picture at the beginning is useful and practical.

2. **Panorama, not close up.** Keep your eyes and mind in panorama mode whenever possible – like the wide photo-graphic panorama mode on your phone or camera. It's about scanning and taking in the wider view. It makes your brain happier, as if you're scanning for prey, lunch or members of your cave community. Diving down, down, down into all of the information and details is a sure-fire way to bring on overload and overwhelm if you're not prepared for it. Argh!

3. **Empty the load:** take a break when you're 'full'. If you've been listening, reading, absorbing, or digesting information for a while, take a break from it, no matter how much you think you should 'push on'. This relief is ... relieving. Even small slivers of a break can 'empty your load,' giving you time to clean up and get ready for the next delivery.

4. **Externalise:** just as visualising invisible work was a powerful technique in Part 2 in The Load of Work, it's practical and useful here too. Stop trying to store or remember so much inside your mind, internally. Store information outside

yourself where possible. If you don't need to remember it, don't.

5. **Start fresh:** tomorrow is a new day to try again. If today was a bit of a disaster or you were overloaded and overwhelmed, you get to clean the slate and try again tomorrow. Your brain loves to tidy things up while you're asleep. Can you 'call it a day' and start afresh tomorrow and let your brain do the housekeeping overnight?

Irrelevant Information
(Catch information)

How do you tell whether you can trust someone you've just met? When we think someone is down to earth, how do we really know? If we have a suspicious feeling or sense about something, how do we determine that?

Many people praise and rely on the power of their intuition. That deep internal knowing, the voice that quietly says, 'Yes, this,' or that feeling you have in your gut and you 'just know'.

These hard to explain but strong sensations we experience are made up of a collection of a small cues and clues:

☆ The *cues* are little signs from our body, processed by our brain.

☆ The *clues* are things we see or sense.

When we bring them together, we create a picture or make a decision based on a possibility ... and we go for it. We say yes or no.

But HOW do we do it? Out of all of the information coming in through our senses, how do we make sense when we really need to, so we know what to do ... and what *not* to do?

It's right there in the name of sensemaking. We sense information, experiences and feelings through our senses. Our powerful tools of vision, hearing, smell, touch and taste work seamlessly together to collect information and then it's assessed, analysed and evaluated by the brain so we can decide what to do next. It's like the job of an interpreter, decoding technical information or another language into our own.

But of all that information coming in, what do we take notice of *the most*?

This is our keen ability to **discern information**. To be able to detect, recognise and pick apart from other information that which is meaningful and valuable and that which is ... well, waffle, wasteful or wishy washy.

> *'I just knew she would be trouble', said Belinda after she fired her office assistant, Lee, who she hired four weeks earlier. Belinda's business prepared floral and fruit hampers for exclusive events, clients and hotels. As her small business was growing, Belinda needed some more hands at work, not just for the administration side of things, but to help with the hands-on work of selecting items for hampers and packing and delivering them.*

But after just a day or two, stock levels were lower than they should have been and Belinda questioned, 'How could it be Lee, the new recruit? Surely she would be on her best behaviour in a new job?'

Plenty of clues led to Lee. No one else had access to the stock, and some numbers had been altered on stock lists. The bottom line was, Belinda was missing stock and she just knew Lee had something to do with it.

Discerning information means we have an ability to pick and choose what we take notice of. Even though Belinda's work was overwhelmingly busy, she was still able to pick up on some of the cues that indicated all wasn't as it should be.

When we are drowning in it, swamped by emotions, thinking, information, tasks or to-dos, we can be less alert or less observant. Things slip by us. And other things we'd normally notice we may miss all together. Our ability to discern isn't as sharp as it could be. And this is a problem of overwhelm. We simply don't have the attention or resources to pick up on everything. Things will fall through the cracks or we will be oblivious and none the wiser.

Eve was blindsided by her husband's call; he said it was over and he wanted a divorce. 'What the fuck?!' she screamed at him, while thinking to herself, 'How did I miss that?' Rather than thinking she really was blindsided, she considered that perhaps there had been signs, but she hadn't picked up on them or hadn't picked them apart from all of the other things going on in their lives.

One night when Eve was catching up for a wine and pasta at her friend Inga's place, Inga handed her a copy of the book *Uncoupling: Turning Points in Intimate Relationships*. 'Don't go all Gwyneth on me, Inga!' said Eve, referring to the 'conscious uncoupling' phrase made famous by actor Gwyneth Paltrow and Coldplay band front man Chris Martin during their separation and divorce.

'Give it a chance,' pleaded Inga. 'It's got some amazing insights and it certainly helped me when I separated from husband number one!'

Eve took the book and started reading it the next morning over breakfast. It was a research-backed summary of what people go through as they feel like, decide to and then ultimately announce their desire to leave a relationship and 'uncouple'. The thing is, one party of the relationship is usually going this course, while the other is completely oblivious.

The call for a separation is a shock, a blindside, and 'I didn't see it coming,' is a common refrain. But once the shocking news has landed, we get to look back over the past weeks, months and years and realise that a number of cues and clues do in fact all add up and make sense. We look back and make sense. Sensemaking, right? Perhaps we didn't see it at the time or didn't realise it or didn't want to know it.

Our ability to discern some of these micro-slivers of information has been blunted by the busyness of life. We simply don't pick up the threads or routines that might make us wonder or notice what's changed in our relationships.

Because it's a shock, the next phases are about attempting to rebalance the relationship, to 'talk it through', 'try again' or to 'change'. But what if the uncoupled one has decided, moved on mentally and is ready to launch into their next phase … without you?

The collapse of a long-term relationship is rarely, truly a surprise, at least to one of the parties. It's been a process of thinking and deciding. But it's the announcement to the other party that is the shock and the surprise. Completely overwhelming.

Blinded by life

Overwhelming information and emotions can blind us and block the vital intuitive hunches and insights we are usually able to pick up on, make sense of and trust, especially when we aren't overwhelmed.

This sensemaking that we do, detective-like work, is akin to the big information board in episodes of CSI Miami or other top crime shows. Strings connecting images, evidence, documents and photos help the detectives work out what's going on and where to look next.

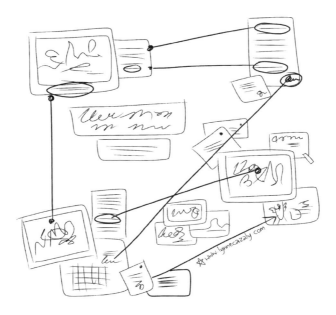

They're often swamped with information. There are witness testimonies and reports or statements, accounts from victims, interviews with suspects and details, details, details – like CCTV footage, employment records, telephone data and banking transactions. From all of this information they choose, select, distinguish and pick out the information that will build their case or solve their crime by the shortest and most accurate route.

How do they know? How do they select *some* information and yet leave others?

This is discernment in action. It's not a 'yes' to everything. And they're consciously and unconsciously doing it every day as a natural part of their job. They may well be highly trained and have years of experience, plus they have a team of investigative smarts working together.

Our individual sensemaking skills are often about us, working alone, and may be just the basic skills we've grown up with. We can tell a red traffic light from a green one. We can tell when a car is travelling fast or slow. We know to slightly speed up as we cross the road as we can judge how fast the vehicle will be travelling and whether it will collide with us or not.

These micro judgements and measurements are going on all day, in every action, conversation and decision. We are looking out for our own safety and survival, taking information in from our surrounds and deciding which bits are worth thinking about and acting on, and which bits are worth dismissing or disposing of. Our survival depends on it!

Extending and developing our sensemaking abilities makes sense. If we can be smarter about what we notice, and what information we take in, surely that can help us arrive at better decisions, notice things sooner, adapt quicker and live a wholly more satisfying, smooth and fulfilling life.

We have our natural abilities developed during our upbringing, but it's never too late to refine or tweak or sharpen our skills. After all, it's often the crusty old investigator or detective who brings their 'time in the game' to bear on solving the case!

Catch the relevance

When you're presented with a lot of information and decide to take notes, say, in a meeting or important conversation, don't write everything down. But do write something down. Not everything matters, yet some of it does. Don't trust your quick-filling sponge (brain) to remember it all or recall it all, but do leave some clues so it can collect the threads and identify key points, later, when you might really need it.

And do write. Tapping on keys doesn't aid in recall, sensemaking and processing as well as we think it might, even though it's an easy thing to do. And if you must type things out, review them afterwards to make greater sense and meaning of them.

Advance or colour

Directors and producers of improvised stage shows might guide a performer to either 'advance' the story, to progress it and move it along, or to 'colour' it.

Colouring it gives more detail, provides more facts, figures and depth. Identify whether the information you're dealing with is advancing or progressing an idea you're working on or is simply colouring it and collecting more detail.

Capturing more and more information will only lead us towards overload and overwhelm. There's a balance here: not so little that we're relying on our brain to do everything; not so much that we are playing 'court reporter' trying to transcribe what was said, or document everything that is said.

Takeaways

1. **Notice what you're noticing.** Being aware, mindful and conscious keeps us tuned in. We don't need to stay hyper alert, but softly mindful is how I like to think of it.

2. **Spot patterns and trends.** When you do notice something, consider if it's part of a matching set. Sensemaking is about connecting several dots, not just one!

3. **Don't believe everything you think.** A contrast to sense-making and discerning is the conspiracy theory approach, where we THINK things are connected but they're not. Ask questions. Get another person's perspective: are you being overly critical, sensitive or judgemental when there's nothing there?

4. **Test things out and take heed of experiment results.** Test out your thinking. Run an experiment. Collect the numbers.

5. **Build your skills and capabilities.** Become more discerning. Like a wine taster who has been at the sniffing, sipping and spitting for years, they often know a great wine when they see it. Or smell it. Their senses are highly tuned and they trust the information their senses are sending them. You can too.

Heavy Information
(Release the pressure)

The load of information is made up of more than just a quantity of information; we also add to the load with our internal dialogue or inner critic. This inner voice is another addition to the load we're trying to carry. It's another channel we're potentially tuned in to.

My inner critic said I wouldn't be too good at writing this part of the book. Heck, it was telling me I wasn't going to be able to write the whole book, not just this section.

The irony of this is both curious and overwhelming.

My inner critic was saying, 'What do you know about inner critics? Who are you to write about this topic? You haven't done enough research on it! Who do you think you are, writing about what could be a psychological science of our inner critic?' and on and on.

And there you have it, an example of how the inner critic shows up and dashes and smashes our thoughts, views and opinions making immediate judgments and assessments 1.7 seconds after we decide to take on a task or activity, whether it's bold and creative or simple and straightforward. That annoying inner critic is based on so little accurate data or valid information that I wonder why we take any notice of it at all. But it is additional information anyway!

While opinions are valid because they are our own, perhaps the opinions from our inner critic need to be called into question more often than they are. We listen to ourselves too much. Mainly because it does not SHUT UP! It can be unrelenting, always present, always travelling with us, walking around with us, sleeping with us. It's providing an ongoing commentary and an endless private internal podcast interview from a broadcaster we never engaged, booked or tuned in to.

Often referred to as our inner dialogue, I would say it's more of an inner monologue. It is often only one voice talking – although I know I sometimes have an argument or debate with my inner critic. In the main though, it is not a dialogue – it's a monologue, a preaching and a ranting from an uninvited guest. No one else seems to get a word in. It's all one way. A rant or ramble of never-ending opinions, dramatisations and exaggerations that are simply not true.

They're an intruder and they're not welcome at all despite us leaving the front door open. It's just like when my neighbour Eleanor baked a beautiful, rich fruit cake last Christmas and her neighbour's over-weight yet apparently starving Golden Labrador dog jumped the fence … well, it walked through the hole in the fence, smashed through the back door … well, it walked through the already open back door, placed its two golden paws onto the bench and swiped the warm fruity cake in its slobbering dog choppers and then made itself comfortable on the floor and made a meal of it. Happy as a Labrador with food!

It's that easy for our inner critic to join in because we rarely lock it out. We leave the door open and in it comes and we can become a kind of hostage to its ramblings.

If you've been at a party or a networking event and been 'bailed up' by the non-stop talker who loves to talk about themselves, the inner critic is like that: bailing us up and non-stop talking at ourselves.

Danielle Krysa, author of *Your Inner Critic is a Big Jerk,* shares four 'buckets of lies' we tell ourselves. While Krysa's book is directed at those producing creative work, the lies are easily recognisable in many people's internal narrative.

They are:

- ☆ Fear (e.g., 'I'm so afraid of failing,' or 'It won't turn out the way I imagined anyway.')

- ☆ The Blame Game (e.g., 'The cat was sleeping on my computer, so I couldn't finish the project.')

- ☆ Environment Issues (e.g., 'I can't concentrate with my house so messy,' or 'The light isn't right.')

and

- ☆ Time (e.g., 'I need more than 30 minutes to make anything worthwhile,' or 'There's no point in starting now because I'll have to stop in three hours …')

All of our internal chatter adds so much more to our load than it warrants.

An additional and unnecessary load

My inner critic was giving me a serve earlier today.

I was leading an online workshop this morning and noticed that I was making up stories about the participants and what they thought of the workshop. One of them didn't look too engaged and so I – actually, my inner critic – thought she was feeling disinterested and that the workshop was unhelpful. Another person looked completely bored and so I – oh, my inner critic – thought he believed the workshop was a waste of his time. A third person didn't have their web-camera on and so my inner critic told me they didn't even want to be there, let alone make eye contact.

How did I know any of this was true?

Well, my inner critic told me, didn't they?

But why would I listen to this? Why should I? How could I even believe this? Were we ever taught, 'Now, always listen to your inner critic because they are right.'? Yet here we all are, paying attention and unquestioningly accepting the words of our inner storyteller.

At the end of the workshop, when the first participant, said, 'Thank you, this has been really helpful,' it surprised me because it was not the vibe I was getting, or the vibe my inner critic was commenting on.

What is a vibe anyway? It is only our construction of a situation and our application of our own fears and filters.

In online meetings there is an extreme lack of non-verbal feedback that we might normally get in a face-to-face meeting and this has probably fired up and given our inner critic an inflated sense of importance. 'Now you're not getting the full story, Lynne, so here, let me make some stuff up for you!' Argh!

Dr Susan David, the author of *Emotional Agility,* says, 'our thoughts come fully accessorised with visual images, symbols, judgement, inferences, abstractions and actions. This gives our mental life a vibrant intensity, but it can also take away our objectivity and leave us at the mercy of our intrusive ideas – whether they're true or not.'

Sensemaking the inner critic

Just as we can pause on our overwhelm (from Part 1) and visualise our workload (from Part 2), we don't pause nearly enough to make sense of or question our inner critic, so when we do, wow … look out! Sensemaking can give us a moment to look back and get some hindsight. We can call the critic's validity into question, ask it for factual information and demand it provide us with some cold, hard evidence to support its ridiculous claims! This is good sensemaking.

And once we do this pausing, we begin to focus more on the moment of what we are doing and less on what we are worrying about, what people think, whether we're good enough.

It happens whenever we get nervous: a first date, a client meeting, a job interview, a parent-teacher meeting. With nerves come a serving of the inner critic and we focus so much on ourselves and the inner voice and not enough on what's actually going on – the date, the client, the job role, how your child is going at school.

Danielle Krysa, the author of *Your Inner Critic is a Big Jerk*, suggests we give it a new name, believing that it's tough to 'turn a phrase that is 50 percent "critic" into anything remotely warm and fuzzy.' Some people, she says, refer to the inner critic as 'Mini Me', 'that voice', 'the opponent' or her favourite, a name used by a friend … 'Arlo'. That's the name of the inner critic … Arlo. In this way, there is some distance between ourselves and the critic; it's not all tied up, swarming about in our heads. In fact, as Krysa suggests, you might even be able to become friends with this renamed and relabelled identity.

When I think about what my
inner critic does, I find it's
better to rename it as
an inner commentator,
because it is rarely
providing useful information,
and more likely to be providing an
ongoing commentary. Yes … just like a sports commentating
team on TV.

A sports commentator calls every move and throws in some opinions, judgements, assumptions and a few guesses!

Like this example from a recent game of tennis: *'This isn't a good
day for Williamson; look, they've lost focus, they look disorganised,
they just don't have the goods!'*

Commentary is laden with opinions. If it was factual reporting from
the sidelines, different matter. Like this one from the Australian
Open. *'That's six winners Williamson has achieved in this first set.
Add that to the 78% of first serves and this is a stronger performance than last week's match.'*

Ok, now that's a commentary that could be useful in a job interview
or a first date.

The power of narration

Plenty of films and TV series are supported and viewed through the
eyes of a narrator. They connect the dots of scenes and are quite

efficient (cheap) for filmmakers to use because they link potentially disconnected ideas.

The Broadway musical *Rock of Ages* has a key character Lonny Barnett who was the narrator, helping link scenes of the stage show together so they made sense.

The *Rocky Horror Picture Show* has a narrator.

Carrie Bradshaw, the character played by Sarah Jessica Parker narrates *Sex and the City*.

Star Trek's narrator is Captain Kirk.

Meredith Grey narrates *Grey's Anatomy*.

Gossip Girl is narrated by an anonymous character, voiced by actress Kristen Bell.

The *Deadpool* films are humorously narrated by Ryan Reynolds' character.

In all of these situations, the narrator keeps the drama going and keeps the story alive. They keep the audience hooked, our eyeballs focused on the screen, buying in to every step of the story, investing our emotions in the plot, characters and drama.

This is exactly what our inner critic commentator is doing, driven to keep the drama going. This gives us something to worry about and to fight for ... we fight for survival after all.

But remember, just like the commentary for a sporting event, if it gets annoying, we can press 'mute' and 'just take the vision, hold the audio, thanks'.

Processing and sensemaking

As we experience situations, challenging or otherwise, we are taking information and micro-cues from people, objects and the environment we are in, connecting this information to make sense and meaning of it.

We also take slivers of information, thoughts, observations and ideas and piece them together like a kind of mystery investigator or crime scene whodunnit.

We are constantly doing this. In every situation in life, we are trying to understand it and make sense of what is happening. We might be trying to understand the things that are difficult to understand and so our inner commentator/narrator steps in to provide some drama, meaning and character development for the audience!

When there is a lack of information for us to make sense of, we fill in the gaps. My optometrist, Ian – who also wears glasses – was telling me about this at a recent eye test because it is exactly how our eyes work. Every mammal, including humans, has a 'blind spot' where the optic nerve connects to the back of the eye, and some people experience other spots of diminished vision resulting from damage to their visual system, called scotomas. The two holes on the front of our face and the intricate technology that operates them can't truly see the full scene that we are looking at. Even though the picture looks completely valid to us, there are pieces of the image that are brain is just making up! We're not really seeing what is there. At least not all of it. Our brain fills in the gaps and makes some assumptions about what else is in the picture.

The same thing happens with our brain providing us with feedback of what is going on. Your inner commentator may not be on air and broadcasting all the time, but it is there, ready to jump in and provide the often unwelcome, unhelpful and uninspiring 'special comments' from the media broadcast box (the brain) about what it *thinks* is going on.

'Let's now cross to the commentary team and hear about how Louisa is going with her job interview …

'Well, that's been a disappointing start when she stood up and tripped on the carpet edging. She struggled a bit picking up her handbag even though it was only sitting on the floor and then her hair fell across her face. Hmmm, poor effort, she could have – SHOULD have – blow-dried that part of her hair more effectively and some hair spray – what about some HAIR SPRAY? – to keep those pieces in place. What will they

think of her? She's made her way into the interview room and now it's awkward, she's hesitating about where to sit and they'll think she's indecisive and I believe if she can't even decide where to sit in a meeting room then how the hell will she be able to decide on thousands of dollars in a budget? This is a disappointing performance from Louisa today and the interview hasn't even really got underway. She may have already blown it with these early moves ... as we know, you don't get a second chance to make a first impression. We'll cross back later for how she's coped with the, "Tell us a little about yourself," interview question. Based on her recent form, I'm not feeling optimistic about how she'll handle it. Back to you in the studio.'

What our inner commentator says may not be true. It's most likely not true. It's a fictitious and dramatised account of every little thing. This is our ego trying to protect us from danger. It's to save us so that we don't look foolish and mess up. It's really saying, 'Hey, be careful out there. Bad stuff could happen.'

and tripped on the carpet edging. She struggled a bit picki up her handbag even though it was only sitting on the floor then her hair fell across her face. Hmmm, poor effort, she cc ve – SHOULD have – blow-dried that part of he ly and some hair sprau

Argh!

Yes, bad stuff can happen, but tuning in to the endless critical commentary of our inner monologue, dialogue, commentator, narrator and critic absolutely adds to our information overload, and in turn, can lead us to a state of overwhelm.

Releasing the pressure

We can't work or think forever, or continuously. We need to pause, stop, rest and recover. This is emptying the load, releasing the pressure, focus and attention we've been using.

At some point – or ideally, several points throughout the day – we need to slip into unfocused time.

'Strategic unfocus', as Srini Pillay, author of *Tinker, Dabble, Doodle, Try: Unlock the Power of the Unfocused Mind* labels it, is the ideal way to rest and recover during the day. When things start getting overwhelming, he says, 'go for a walk to make connections' in your brain of the information and work you've just been doing and re-establish a kind of control by just taking in your local surroundings, not the impossible everything of … everything!

Many people enjoy meditation, music, relaxation, walking the dog, reading, having a cup of coffee or tea, chatting to a friend, moving the body by stretching or simply changing their position, state and mind. All of these things help us release the pressure we've been carrying and ready us for the next load.

Above all, to release the load, we've got to allow more buffer and less pressure. That is, putting a small gap in between back-to-back meetings and not 'pushing on' or 'working through' breaks such as lunchtime in the belief it's better for productivity. It's just not!

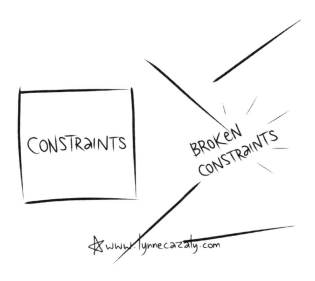

CONSTRAINTS

BROKEN CONSTRAINTS

www.lynnecazaly.com

And when you're timeboxing (from Part 2 The Load of Work, Focus on the Task), when the timer goes off, the timebox is finished, release the pressure there too! Take a break. Get up and move, do something else, somewhere else – even for a few minutes – before you embark on the next timebox. This pressure release helps with emptying our cognitive load and enables us to pay greater attention over a longer period of time. I know it can be hard to stop, particularly if you feel like 'I'm on a roll, I'm in flow'. Sometimes I'll set another timebox for another 10, 15 or 25 minutes, and THEN release the pressure with a break.

Humans work quite well within constraints, boundaries and borders – like a sandbox or a timebox. We work even better when the constraints are released when the task is done or the responsibility is no longer on us. Relax. Exhale. Rest. Recover. It just makes sense.

Takeaways

1. **Fiction not fact.** Know the narrative you're hearing or listening to is incomplete and fictitious, dramatised and exaggerated.

2. **There is a story emerging.** What is it? Take what you're seeing or hearing as some early indicators and not the full story. It's like a first layer of an onion; the first coat of paint.

3. **Gather some more facts.** Before you decide whether anything the inner commentator is saying is valid, check it against some data. What did the feedback results say? What were the end of quarter statistics? Check against the actuals. That first sensemaking question is helpful: what's going on?

4. **Seek out more than a commentator's opinion.** Check with a trusted friend or a wise mentor to test and validate your thinking.

5. **What do you need to do about it?** Consider the second sensemaking question to plan your next actions.

Sensemaking the Information

Sensemaking:

What is going on ?

and

What do I need
to do about it ?

☆www.lynnecazaly.com

1. Filter

Filter. It means, as a verb, 'to pass through a device to remove unwanted material'. It's about clarifying, cleaning up and refining. Of all the information coming at you, consider the filter you're applying. Be conscious, more conscious of filtering information, rather than just trying to 'take it all in'.

You can filter by:

- scanning information

- looking for key themes

- focusing on relevant points

- keeping the bigger context in mind

- telling yourself what you're 'keeping an eye out for'.

Just 'tuning in' to the reason why you're reading, looking, listening to something is often enough focused attention for us to pick up cues and clues and start the filtering process.

2. Catch

Apply the technique of externalising information by capturing or catching some of what you're seeing, reading or listening to. You don't need to capture or write it all, but do write something. The act of capturing helps us retain focus, keeps us engaged and helps ward off the rising waters of overwhelm.

And go for more of a map, a sensemaking map, than a long list of words that might be difficult to make sense of later. Our brain loves pictures and imagery; creating a visual map of the important and relevant pieces of information will help both in the storage and retrieving processes.

Use one of these templates if you like, or create your own. There are no rules for making maps of information but simply to make a map, whatever it looks like.

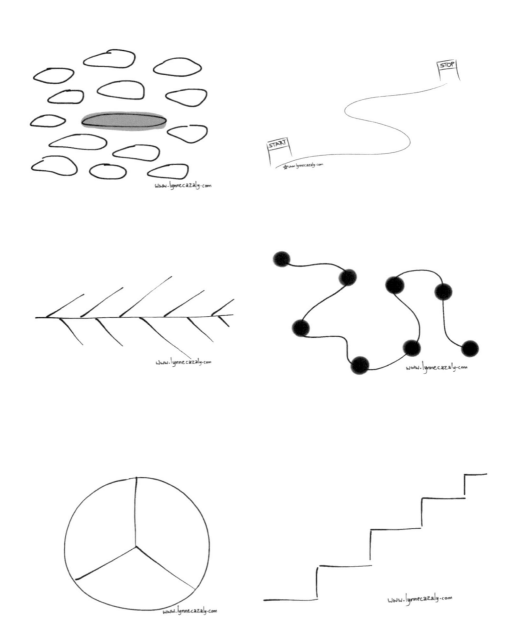

3 Release

Stop paying attention. At the end of the task, reading, listening, focusing, remember to release the pressure of your attention. Do something else. Get up. Move. Go over there, look at something else and give yourself the vital break to recover ... even if it's just a few minutes.

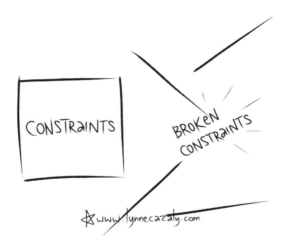

CONSTRAINTS

BROKEN CONSTRAINTS

www.lynnecazaly.com

Something more to soothe

There's also a brilliant benefit of listening to nature when releasing the pressure – even if you can't have nature near you. Storms and rain, wind and waves, birds and trees!

Many, many YouTube tracks are available – some for 8+ hours' listening – for long-term background noise or for a short focused burst if you're reading or working on a specific task or project. We don't always have to choose music, media or podcasts … or people! There's plenty of calmer and calming alternatives for overwhelm.

I find the rain and thunder sound effects calm me and help me sleep, as does the sound of the waves crashing on a beach.

This is about us self-soothing or self-managing, being able to shift our state and manage our moods. To self-soothe is a capability and there are many new capabilities we have to help manage ourselves every day and outsmart the potential rising overwhelm.

the OVERWHELM	❶ PaUSe	❷ LoCaTe	❸ ReLaBeL
	Re-define the overwhelm		
the WORK	❹ VIZUaLISe	❺ PRIORITISe	❻ FOCUS
	Re-design the work		
the INFoRMaTION	❼ FILTeR	❽ CaTCH	❾ ReLeaSe
	Re-direct your attention ☆www.lynnecazaly.com		

Download these templates and other resources at
www.lynnecazaly.com.au/argh

Some Final Words About Sensemaking

Make sense as you go

In a meeting recently I saw a colleague write up more than five pages of notes. The next day they said how confused they felt about it all.

What were all the notes about then?

Sometimes we can capture content others are delivering, thinking we're doing well, getting all of that information down. But it can end up meaning nothing to us later. We don't seem to be able to find what the key points were or what the essence of it was.

As I chatted with my colleague later and we reviewed their notes, they were words and phrases underlined. These were the key things they heard. But later, none of it really made much sense. There was no synthesis, distilling, connections or conclusions. The notes were parts of sentences.

In sensemaking, it helps to pause, listen, make sense of what's going on, and write that down. It is habit (and fear) that drives us to write it all down like a court reporter! But we don't need to write it all.

So make sense as you go, capture information as it makes sense to you. Go for distilling information rather than transcribing it!

Write something down

When we're in say, a training program, a complex or important meeting or at a conference, remember ... we don't need to write it ALL down. But we do need to write something.

What to write? Listen and look out for:

- ☆ Key points that feel important to you.

- ☆ Changes in a speaker or presenter's tone. Often the person or people we're with will give us 'signposts' of importance. They'll EMPHASISE something with loudness, or s-l-o-w-i-n-g every word down to really make sure we've heard it.

- ☆ Nuggets and quotable quotes. The media love 'key messages', those 25 words or less statements. Think of what would fit on a t-shirt as a slogan or on a bumper sticker on the back of a car. What might make a good meme on social media? These are examples of nuggets.

- ☆ Directions to something or somewhere else. Sometimes we are given names, places, books, resources, websites to check on for further information. They're a good catch if you do need to 'go back' and find out more.

To all you 'sponges' reading this who sit in meetings and conferences thinking you can 'soak it all up', without actively capturing any notes ... um, you can't. This is precisely a behaviour that can worsen cognitive overload and lead us to feel overwhelmed.

We do nothing, sitting passively, letting information supposedly flow over or through us, thinking we'll remember it and absorb it. But like all sponges, we fill up – and sooner than we think.

A participant in a workshop sat all day with arms crossed, nothing written down. 'I can remember it,' she said, 'I have a photographic memory.' But she didn't remember it and later showed how she'd missed plenty. She just wasn't able to make sense, connect the dots or get the most out of the session. Given her leadership role, number of direct reports and her responsibility in the organisation, it was poor role modelling and self-management.

It's a foolish denial – and a cognitive load coping error – to not write something.

Don't write everything.

And don't writing nothing.

But absolutely ... write something. Your brain will hook on to what you have captured and help you retrieve other information associated with it.

Make sense at the end of the day

The overwhelm of back-to-back meetings is real. So. Much. Content. Words and questions and people and ideas and still more meetings.

Our cognitive load takes a beating as we shove more information into our already overloaded brain. It's hard work.

In between meetings is the ideal time to pause, review, move and have a kind of 'reset', ready for the next meeting.

Deliberately.

And then at the end of the day, another pause. Review and clear the slate for the transition to social, family or home activities.

Otherwise, it can get messy and the overloaded feeling takes longer to process naturally, automatically, organically. Do it deliberately.

Empty the load – between meetings if you can; and absolutely at the end of the working day. (And the end of the week too!)

Stop squirrelling information

One issue is how we squirrel away information, intent on working on it 'later', reviewing it, keeping it, having it. Think … at a conference where a tonne of information is presented via PowerPoint. How often have you got your phone out and taken a photo of a slide?

We're creating a 'rework' problem though, collecting information we think we may possibly need, perhaps, maybe.

'It looks valuable; I'll capture it.' It's inefficient and delays the sensemaking task until 'later'. That's yet another thing for 'later'!

Research by Julia S. Soares and Benjamin C. Storm published in the *Journal of Applied Research in Memory and Cognition* confirms our memories and recall are NOT enhanced by these photos. In 'Forget in a Flash: A Further Investigation of the Photo-Taking-Impairment Effect' the researchers confirm that when we think we're offloading the memory work to a camera, our memories of situations, events and observations fade faster.

This is often seen at a conference when a speaker presents slides of information and a sea of cameras from the audience rise as one, snapping photos of the slides.

We're better off working with the information (listening, reading, thinking, writing … sensemaking) at the time, in the moment, even though it feels good to take photos.

We think we feel calmer capturing the moment, but we're actually adding to the big problem that is our cognitive overload. Forget the photo. Make sense in the moment.

Summary

Overwhelm is a personal place, an often individual space ... made from our own unique experiences, situations and responses. While for some, overwhelm can be a familiar, debilitating and frequent state to be in, for others it's a surprise or shock when it arrives, unexpectedly.

As the world continues to serve up situations that we may not be prepared for, we are being challenged to work out what's going on and what we need to do about it.

To understand and appreciate what our own version of overwhelm is, in an ever-challenging world is a powerful and empowering position to be in.

How can we not fight or resist the overwhelm ... or even manage it, but rather make sense of it, every time?

Our powers of sensemaking already exist, and with some additional tools, techniques and templates we can make sense sooner, get on the other side of the experiences we're in and understand what's going on.

Understanding the dangers of prolonged and unresolved over-whelm is a wake-up call. Burn-out is waiting, along with a host of physical, psychological and emotional woes. It serves us and those we live, work and play with to make sense and act on overwhelm.

The loads we carry

Overwhelm may well be arriving not because of one thing, but as a result of many things, piled up on one another.

Redefining overwhelm is a big part of outsmarting it. Instead of 'I'm so overwhelmed', remember that redefining it for what it is, and what it means to you, is a brilliant and effective step.

And realising that our emotional overwhelm could be made up of a heavy workload, plus an insurmountable pile of information to catch up on is liberating too. Now we are pulling the pieces apart, getting to make sense of it.

As you keep an eye on the Ladder of Overwhelm, watch out for how you can be spending less time drowning, struggling and juggling, and more time understanding, progressing and achieving.

The load of work

The world of work keeps changing and with it, the boundaries between home and work, roles of work ... even the definition of what is work for us. When we allow work to remain 'inside' and internalised, we are headed for overwhelm. When we try to do too many things at once, switching between them, we could be headed for overwhelm. And when we lose focus and drop our attention from the task at hand, again, we can be inviting overwhelm.

Visualise the work.
Prioritise the work.
Focus on the task.

The load of information

More of it is coming … information. There's more coming via email inboxes, attachments, social media, media generally, communication, correspondence, mail and directly from people's mouths … the words we speak. We can't take it all in so to filter is a must. What do you need to pay attention to, and why? Catch that which is important, relevant, useful, helpful – not everything, but also, not nothing! Catch something, externalising it out of your mind and onto a page, onto a map. Any kind of map.

And when the tough work is done, the timebox is up or the focus is waning, release the pressure of attention. Take a break. Take in a tune or a sound, or some nature, or a human.

Sensemaking is a skill already available to us; now, combined with a greater understanding of our overwhelm, some effective working techniques and some cognitive load coping skills, we've got three BIG perspectives of overwhelm covered.

The outsmarting of overwhelm is well underway. Keep going. Get smarter by refining your practices, practicing the skills, sharing them with others and telling your story of the effects of how over-whelm is not so overwhelming anymore.

I'd love you to join in the community, download more resources and dive in to the supports, templates and conversations that are continuing on 'Argh! Too Much Information, Not Enough Brain: A Practical Guide to Outsmarting Overwhelm'.

Next Steps

Take a walk through this checklist to see if there are some of the practices you could focus on, revisit, or try out.

- ☐ I make sustainable choices before I'm overwhelmed.

- ☐ I'm trying out some of the sensemaking templates.

- ☐ I ask myself what's going on and what do I need to do about it.

- ☐ I recognise overwhelm when it approaches.

- ☐ I redefine overwhelm.

- ☐ I relabel what is really going on for me.

- ☐ I consider the meaning of tasks, chores or projects and how that might impact my experience of overwhelm.

- ☐ I understand what's contributing to my experiences of overload.

- ☐ I visualise my workload.

- ☐ I use a Kanban board or other external tool to capture all of the tasks in my backlog.

- ☐ I reduce multitasking.

- ☐ I reduce switching rapidly between tasks.

- ☐ I reduce the number of tasks I am working on, my work in progress.

- ☐ I notice what distracts me.

- ☐ I focus my attention using timeboxing.

- ☐ I focus my attention prior to taking in information.

- ☐ I don't try and write everything down.

- ☐ I do write something down.

- ☐ I release the pressure after a timebox or focused period of time.

- ☐ I remind myself to 'empty my truck' and rest my brain.

- ☐ I notice when I defer or postpone taking a break.

- ☐ I enjoy the relief of the release of focused attention.

More Resources

Resources:

1. In denial about overwhelm?

Do you feel exhausted and overwhelmed, but you're still telling yourself that this is absolutely a-ok, totally normal, and you're handling everything on your massive to-do list amazingly?

If not, and you think you could possibly, maybe wonder if you really do experience overwhelm or overload, check out this list; do any of these seem or feel familiar?

overcome	affected	submerged
compressed	crushed	surprised
swamped	engulfed	beaten
beat	defeated	astonished
overpowered	moved	flabbergasted
devastated	thunderstruck	stunned
wrecked	aghast	astounded
shocked	depressed	overpowered
confused	dumbfounded	confounded

deluged   perplexed   downtrodden
distressed   dazed   flooded
concerned   burdened
overworked   disrupted

OK, not all of them at once, but some of those have a real punch about them! And overwhelm can do this to us. If you notice yourself experiencing any of these, it could be you've already relabelled your overwhelm – which is what we were talking about in Part 1. And if you've got a plan for how you're going to respond, that's good too. Making sense of overload and overwhelm is a wonderful practice and precursor to decision making. And once decisions are made, they're easier for us to act on.

2. Triggers and relievers

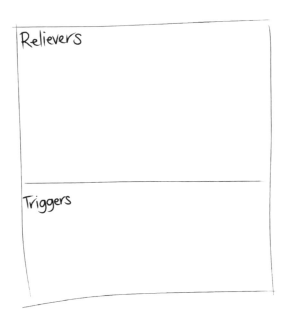

Relievers

Triggers

Create your own triggers and relievers list.

That is, the stuff that you KNOW helps relieve or reduce over-whelm for you ... and the stuff that you know can add to, cause or contribute to it.

This is the worksheet I use as my go-to. If I'm feeling overwhelmed, I check if any of the things that are going on are on my **triggers** list. It's a nice validation in a way; I'm not going crazy, it's just some of the stuff that adds up to the feeling of overload or overwhelm for me.

And then there is the **relievers** part of the sheet. What are the things that I know can work? They may not always work; I might have to try one, two, or three of them to find the one/s that do the trick for 'this' overwhelming and overloading situation.

I keep this page near my desk, pinned on my bookcase, close at hand, so I can check it when I need to.

Download these templates and other resources at
www.lynnecazaly.com.au/argh

Learn with others, share your experiences,
pick up more tips and techniques.

Join the Argh! Community at Lynne Cazaly's Network.

Go to www.lynnecazaly.com.au/argh

References

Auster, Ellen, and Shannon Auster-Weiss. "Conquer Your To-Do List with This Simple Hack." *Harvard Business Review*, 6 Aug. 2020, hbr.org/2020/08/conquer-your-to-do-list-with-this-simple-hack.

Baker, Mitzi. "Music Moves Brain to Pay Attention, Stanford Study Finds." *Stanford Medicine News Center*, Stanford Medicine, 1 Aug. 2007, med.stanford.edu/news/all-news/2007/07/music-moves-brain-to-pay-attention-stanford-study-finds.html.

Barr, Sabrina. "Women Are Still Doing the Majority of Household Chores, Study Finds." *The Independent*, Independent Digital News and Media, 26 July 2019, 09:10, www.independent.co.uk/life-style/women-men-household-chores-domestic-house-gender-norms-a9021586.html.

Benson, Jim, and Tonianne DeMaria. Barry. *Personal Kanban: Mapping Work, Navigating Life*. Createspace Independent Publishing Platform, 2011.

Boyes, Alice. "5 Things to Do When You Feel Overwhelmed by Your Workload." *Harvard Business Review*, Harvard Business Publishing, 6 Aug. 2018, hbr.org/2018/08/5-things-to-do-when-you-feel-overwhelmed-by-your-workload.

Buzan, Tony, and Barry Buzan. *The Mind Map Book*. BBC, 2005.

Cable, Daniel M. *Alive at Work: the Neuroscience of Helping Your People Love What They Do*. Harvard Business Review Press, 2018.

Cainer, Oscar, and Jonathan Cainer. "Cufflinks of Love." *Astrology / Horoscopes – Oscar and Jonathan Cainer's Daily Horoscopes*, 6 Apr. 2021, www.cainer.com/daily-horoscope/.

Chan, K.M., and K. Horneffer. "Emotional Expression and Psychological Symptoms: A Comparison of Writing and Drawing." *The Arts in Psychotherapy*, vol. 33, no. 1, 2006, pp. 26–36., doi:10.1016/j.aip.2005.06.001.

Coffitivity, coffitivity.com/.

"Cognitive Load." *Wikipedia*, Wikimedia Foundation, 25 Mar. 2021, en.wikipedia. org/wiki/Cognitive_load.

Conklin, Emily. "12 Ways That Music Makes You More Productive At Work (Infographic)." *Entrepreneur*, Entrepreneur Media, Inc., 28 Oct. 2017, www. entrepreneur.com/article/303551.

Curran, Thomas, and Andrew P Hill. "Perfectionism Is Increasing, and That's Not Good News." *Harvard Business Review*, Harvard Business Pulishing, 26 Jan. 2018, hbr.org/2018/01/perfectionism-is-increasing-and-thats-not-good-news.

Curtin, Melanie. "Neuroscience Says Listening to This Song Reduces Anxiety by Up to 65 Percent." *Inc.com*, Mansueto Ventures, 30 May 2017, www.inc.com/melanie-curtin/neuroscience-says-listening-to-this-one-song-reduces-anxiety-by-up-to-65-percent.html.

David, Susan. *Emotional Agility: Get Unstuck, Embrace Change and Thrive in Work and Life (Audio Download): Susan David, Claire Gordon-Webster, Penguin Books Ltd: Amazon.com.au: Audible*, Penguin Books Ltd, 23 May 2016.

Deer-Zapier, Joe. "You're Doing Emotional Labor at Work. Here's How to 'Feel' Better." *Fast Company*, Mansueto Ventures, 28 Feb. 2021, 5:00 AM, www.fastcompany. com/90608933/youre-doing-emotional-labor-at-work-heres-how-to-feel-better.

Epstein, Mark. *Advice Not Given: a Guide to Getting over Yourself*. Penguin Books, 2019.

Epstein, Mark. "The Trauma of Being Alive." *The New York Times*, 3 Aug. 2013, www.nytimes.com/2013/08/04/opinion/sunday/the-trauma-of-being-alive.html.

Fidler, Devin. Edited by Susanna Williams, Institute for the Future, 2016, *Future Skills Update and Literature Review*, www.iftf.org/fileadmin/user_upload/downloads/wfi/ACTF_IFTF_FutureSkills-report.pdf.

Flanagan, Kieran, and Dan Gregory. *Forever Skills: the 12 Skills to Future Proof Yourself, Your Team and Your Kids*. Wiley, 2019.

"Gender Equality in the Domestic Division of Labour." *ReviseSociology*, 3 May 2015, revisesociology.com/tag/who-does-the-housework.

Godin, Seth. "Good Intentions (How to Be on Time)." *Seth's Blog*, 11 Jan. 2019, seths.blog/2019/01/good-intentions-how-to-be-on-time/.

Holden, Robert. *Shift Happens!: How to Live an Inspired Life – Starting Right Now!* 1st ed., Hay House, 2011.

"'Infomania' Worse than Marijuana." *BBC News*, 22 Apr. 2005, news.bbc.co.uk/2/hi/uk_news/4471607.stm.

"John Sweller." *Wikipedia*, Wikimedia Foundation, 22 Feb. 2021, en.wikipedia.org/wiki/John_Sweller.

"Kanban (Development)." *Wikipedia*, Wikimedia Foundation, Inc., 24 Mar. 2021, en.wikipedia.org/wiki/Kanban_(development).

Krysa, Danielle. *Your Inner Critic Is a Big Jerk - and Other Truths about Being Creative*. Illustrated ed., Chronicle Books, 2016.

Livni, Ephrat. "Keyboards Are Overrated. Cursive Is Back and It's Making Us Smarter." *Quartz*, Quartz Media, Inc., 25 July 2017, qz.com/1037057/keyboards -are-overrated-cursive-is-back-and-its-making-us-smarter/.

Mackay, Hugh. *What Makes Us Tick?: Making Sense of Who We Are and the Desires That Drive Us*. 1st ed., Hachette Australia, 2013.

Marconi Union. Edited by Lyz Cooper, *A Study Investigating the Relaxation Effects of the Music Track Weightless*, www.britishacademyofsoundtherapy.com/ wp-content/uploads/2019/10/Mindlab-Report-Weightless-Radox-Spa.pdf.

Markovitz, Daniel. "To-Do Lists Don't Work." *Harvard Business Review*, Harvard Business Publishing, 24 Jan. 2012, hbr.org/2012/01/to-do-lists-dont-work.

Mcmunn, Anne, et al. "Gender Divisions of Paid and Unpaid Work in Contemporary UK Couples." *Work, Employment and Society*, vol. 34, no. 2, 25 July 2019, pp. 155–173., doi:10.1177/0950017019862153.

McQuillan, Susan. "Why We Do Bad Things: How to Break a Bad Habit." *Psychology Today*, 24 Apr. 2009, www.psychologytoday.com/au/blog/cravings/200904/ why-we-do-bad-things.

Medina, John. *Brain Rules: 12 Principles for Surviving and Thriving at Work, Home, and School*. Pear Press, 2008.

Mehta, Ravi, et al. "Is Noise Always Bad? Exploring the Effects of Ambient Noise on Creative Cognition." *Journal of Consumer Research*, vol. 39, no. 4, Dec. 2012, pp. 784–799., doi:10.1086/665048.

Merron, Alice. *Burnout Put Me in the Hospital. This Is What I Learned about Healthy Work-Life Balance*. 12 Jan. 2021, www.fastcompany.com/90592663/burnout-put- me-in-the-hospital-this-is-what-i-learned-about-healthy-work-life-balance.

Newman, Kira M. "How Journaling Can Help You in Hard Times." *Greater Good Magazine*, 18 Aug. 2020, greatergood.berkeley.edu/article/item/ how_journaling_can_help_you_in_hard_times.

Patel, Deep. "These 6 Types of Music Are Known to Dramatically Improve Productivity." *Entrepreneur*, Entrepreneur Media, Inc., 9 Jan. 2019, www. entrepreneur.com/article/325492.

Pillay, Srini. "The Ways Your Brain Manages Overload, and How to Improve Them." *Harvard Business Review*, 7 June 2017, hbr.org/2017/06/ the-ways-your-brain-manages-overload-and-how-to-improve-them.

Pozen, Robert C, and Kevin Downey. "What Makes Some People More Productive Than Others." *Harvard Business Review*, Harvard Business Publishing, 28 Mar. 2019, hbr.org/2019/03/what-makes-some-people-more-productive-than-others?utm _campaign=hbr&utm_medium=social&utm_source=twitter.

Smith, D. "Multitasking Undermines Our Efficiency, Study Suggests." *Monitor on Psychology*, Oct. 2001, p. 13, www.apa.org/monitor/oct01/multitask.

Snowmanradio. "Bike Shed 15d06.Jpg." *Wikipedia, The Free Encyclopedia*, 16 Dec. 2006, en.wikipedia.org/wiki/File:Bike_shed_15d06.jpg.

Soares, Julia S, and Benjamin C Storm. "Forget in a Flash: A Further Investigation of the Photo-Taking-Impairment Effect." *Journal of Applied Research in Memory and Cognition*, vol. 7, no. 1, Mar. 2018, pp. 154–160. *Science Direct*, doi:10.1075/ ps.5.3.02chi.audio.2f.

Sweller, John. "Cognitive Load During Problem Solving: Effects on Learning." *Cognitive Science*, vol. 12, no. 2, Apr. 1988, pp. 257–285., doi:10.1207/s15516709 cog1202_4.

Taube, Aaron. "You Lose Up To 25 Minutes Every Time You Respond To An Email." *Business Insider Australia*, 10 Dec. 2014, www.businessinsider.com.au/you-lose-up-to-25-minutes-every-time-you-respond-to-an-email-2014-12?r=US&IR=T.

"The Definitive 100 Most Useful Productivity Tips." *Filtered*, learn.filtered.com/ hubfs/Definitive 100 Most Useful Productivity Hacks.pdf.

Torres, Monica. "The 40 Everyday Horrors That Are Most Stressful to Us." *Ladders*, Ladders, Inc., 12 Oct. 2018, www.theladders.com/career-advice/ the-40-everyday-horrors-that-are-most-stressful-to-us.

Tsaousides, Theo. *Brainblocks: Overcoming the 7 Hidden Barriers to Success.* Prentice Hall Press, 2015.

Treseder, William. "The Two Things Killing Your Ability to Focus." *Harvard Business Review*, Harvard Business Publishing, 3 Aug. 2016, hbr.org/2016/08/ the-two-things-killing-your-ability-to-focus.

Udemy Business. "Udemy In Depth: 2018 Workplace Distraction Report." 2018, research.udemy.com/wp-content/uploads/2018/03/FINAL-Udemy_2018_ Workplace_Distraction_Report.pdf.

Van Wouwe, Jacobus P., editor. "Physical, Psychological and Occupational Consequences of Job Burnout: A Systematic Review of Prospective Studies." *PLoS One*, 2017, doi:10.1371/journal.pone.0185781.

White, Gillian B. "The Alarming, Long-Term Consequences of Workplace Stress." *The Atlantic*, The Atlantic Monthly Group, 12 Feb. 2015, www.theatlantic. com/business/archive/2015/02/the-alarming-long-term-consequences -of-workplace-stress/385397/.

Zao-Sanders, Marc. "How Timeboxing Works and Why It Will Make You More Productive." *Harvard Business Review*, Harvard Business Publishing, 12 Dec. 2018, hbr. org/2018/12/how-timeboxing-works-and-why-it-will-make-you-more-productive.

Zucker, Rebecca. "How to Deal with Constantly Feeling Overwhelmed." *Harvard Business Review*, Harvard Business Publishing, 10 Oct. 2019, hbr.org/2019/10/ how-to-deal-with-constantly-feeling-overwhelmed.

Notes

1   https://revisesociology.com/tag/who-does-the-housework

2   https://hbr.org/2010/05/how-and-why-to-stop-multitaski.html

3   https://www.apa.org/monitor/oct01/multitask

4   https://hbr.org/2010/05/how-and-why-to-stop-multitaski.html)

5   http://news.bbc.co.uk/2/hi/uk_news/4471607.stm

6   https://www.businessinsider.com/you-lose-up-to-25-minutes-every-time-you-respond-to-an-email-2014-12

7   https://www.ics.uci.edu/~gmark/chi08-mark.pdf)

8   https://news.stanford.edu/2009/08/24/multitask-research-study-082409/

9   https://www.sciencedaily.com/releases/2009/10/091019172628.htm

10 https://www.news.com.au/finance/work/careers/university-attrition-rates-why-are-so-many-students-dropping-out/news-story/3e491dd119e1249a5a3763ef8010f8b5

About Lynne Cazaly

Lynne Cazaly helps individuals, teams and businesses transition to better ways of thinking and working.

Lynne is an international keynote speaker, multi-award-winning author and a master facilitator.

She is the author of seven books:

Better Ways of Thinking and Working: How Changing the Way You Do Things, Changes What You Can Do

ish: The Problem with our Pursuit for Perfection and the Life-Changing Practice of Good Enough

Agile-ish: How to Create a Culture of Agility

Leader as Facilitator: How to Engage, Inspire and Get Work Done

Making Sense: A Handbook for the Future of Work

Create Change: How to Apply Innovation in an Era of Uncertainty

Visual Mojo: How to Capture Thinking, Convey Information and Collaborate Using Visuals

Lynne is an experienced radio broadcaster, presenter and producer having presented more than 10,000 hours on-air. Her background is as a communication specialist, having lectured in undergraduate and postgraduate programs in several of Australia's universities and consulting to different industries and sectors on change and transformation.

Lynne can help you think better, make sense of information and handle the realities of workplace overwhelm and information overload with her clever hacks and ingenious processes, tools and methods.

Lynne is an experienced board director and chair and an #avgeek, loving everything aviation, helicopters and air traffic control.

To request more information on how you can work with Lynne, or have her speak at your next event, please email: info@lynnecazaly.com

You can access Lynne Cazaly's Author Page via this link: www.lynnecazaly.com

Facebook.com/lynnecazaly

Twitter.com/lynnecazaly

Instagram.com/lynnecazaly